The Complete
MARRIED

Book

The Complete MARRIED WITH CHILDREN Book

TV's Dysfunctional Family Phenomenon

By Denise Noe

BearManor Media
2017

The Complete Married… With Children *Book:*
TV's Dysfunctional Family Phenomenon

© 2017 Denise Noe

All Rights Reserved.
Reproduction in whole or in part without the author's permission is strictly forbidden.

BearManor Media
P. O. Box 71426
Albany, GA 31708

bearmanormedia.com

Typesetting and layout by John Teehan

Published in the USA by BearManor Media

ISBN—978-1-62933-189-8

DEDICATION

This book is dedicated to three people:
David Dickerson, Alan Joe Dickerson,
and Don Neustadt

TABLE OF CONTENTS

The Upstart Network and the Innovative Writers 1
The Stumbling Block 7
Pilot with a Pow! 9
A First Season Showcases A Show's Freshness 15
A Cast and Crew Starting Out 21
Shaking It Up with Second and Third Seasons 25
Unwanted Publicity Boost: Terry Rakolta 31
Season 4: Grills, Chills, and Doggy Thrills 35
Season 5: Look Alive and Thrive! 39
Season 6: The Show Goes On and How! 43
Season 7: Not Heaven But Truly Seven 47
Season 8: Bundy Life Continues Not-So-Great 51
Season 9: Moye and Leavitt All Down the Line 57
Season 10: In-laws and Other Outrages 63
Season 11: Last But Not Least… 67
End Of A Show, End Of An Era 71
Al vs. Marcy 75
The Lost Episode Is Aired 77
Comical But Compassionate, Liberal But Conservative ... 79
Bibliography 83
Appendix of Married… with Children Episodes 87

THE UPSTART NETWORK AND THE INNOVATIVE WRITERS

FROM THE TIME TELEVISION began as an everyday media in average American homes in the 1950s, replacing radio as the primary personal entertainment medium, the Big Three networks—ABC, NBC, and CBS—had dominated TV. Efforts to launch a fourth network to compete with the Big Three had been notably unsuccessful before FOX started its attempt in the 1980s. However, FOX was determined to carve out a place for itself as a fourth network that would gain a respectable audience share. The Big Three had a forty-year start, so this project was not going to be easy.

To distinguish itself, FOX decided to go for a younger, more liberal, "hipper" audience than that targeted by its competitors. Garth Ancier, not yet 30 years of age, was recruited from NBC to FOX. At NBC, Ancier had been Vice-President of Current Comedy Programs. Ancier turned to writers Ron Leavitt and Michael Moye and asked them to create a situation comedy that would draw in the young and liberal demographic FOX sought.

At least at the time Ancier first hired them, Ron Leavitt and Michael Moye did not look like successful television writers. Both were notably casual in dress and manner. Leavitt was a white man with long, stringy, greasy hair; Moye was a black man whose hair was usually unfashionably unattended-to. Both were often unkempt, and tended toward t-shirts and sloppy jeans. The appearance of the two writers was so slovenly that they were frequently stopped at guard shacks and gates because security officers believed they did not belong there. In fact, the pair often resembled homeless people. Indeed, a homeless man once mistook Leavitt for someone similarly situated and offered Leavitt a sip from a wine bottle. The penniless fellow looked on in astonishment as the sloppily attired but very affluent Leavitt soon stepped into his BMW and drove away. Although given to slovenly attire, both men boasted solid writing credentials, between them having written for such popular TV sitcoms as *Happy Days*, *Laverne & Shirley*, *The Jeffersons*, *Good Times*, and *Diff'rent Strokes*.

In the mid-1980s, the best-known TV family sitcoms were *The Cosby Show*, *Family Ties*, and *Growing Pains*—all sitcoms of the Big Three. These programs featured families that were essentially wholesome and cooperative. The strong, competent, wise parents and "good kid" children had echoes of previous classic sitcom winners such as *Leave It To Beaver*, *The Andy Griffith Show*, *My Three Sons*, and *Father Knows Best*.

The maverick writers were excited by the assignment. Director Gerry Cohen recalls, "They were disgusted by the insipid nature of TV sitcoms." Cohen elaborates that Leavitt and Moye did not want another show in which "everyone's problems are solved in twenty minutes" and ends with "everyone sitting around the dinner table happy."

Recalling the discussions he and Leavitt had, Moye says, "We wanted a sitcom that *wasn't* imitative." In fact, the unofficial working title for the sitcom they were creating was *Not The Cosbys*, because they intended their program to be a contrast to the wholesomeness of that show. They wanted to create television sitcom characters who were at least as flawed, if not more so, than the majority of the people viewing them.

Leavitt and Moye drew the basics of what they wanted for their sitcom from two comedy routines they liked. One was of fat homely comedian Sam Kinison railing against marriage; the other was of fat homely comedienne Roseann Barr railing against marriage. The idea for *Not The Cosbys* was created with Kinison and Barr in mind. The writing partners imagined a show in which Kinison and Barr, who had griped so humorously about marriage, were married to each other. However, neither Kinison nor Barr wanted to act in the projected sitcom.

When *Married... With Children* hit the air, it was widely speculated that the family was named "Bundy" after infamous serial murderer Ted Bundy. However, the writers always insisted that they named the family after the flamboyant bald wrestler King Kong Bundy.

The family as sketched by Leavitt and Moye consisted of an unhappily married couple, a daughter and son, and a dog. Much comic foiling would be offered by a special friendship—and quasi-enmity—with their next-door neighbors.

Gerry Cohen, who directed more *MWC* episodes than anyone else, recalls, "It was so different it was hard to imagine this thing getting on the air and being successful."

Casting is always a top priority for any program since the proper "fit" between performer and role is key to any show's success. With both first choices out, Moye and Leavitt decided they did not want established actors for the leads. They believed that little known actors would be better at defining the characters and being seen by viewers as the characters.

In contrast to Barr, Katey Sagal is conventionally pretty. Although not what Leavitt and Moye had envisioned, they saw in her readings that she possessed an interesting interpretation of Peg

Ed O'Neill understood the resignation vital to the character of Al Bundy

Bundy as a middle-aged woman who yearns to see herself as still the "hot chick" she was in her youth. Sagal recalls that she did not want to play Peg as a slob but as a woman who takes good care of her appearance and wants to be appreciated for it. Thus, she auditioned in colorful tight-fitting capris, large tight belt, and high-heeled shoes. The ensemble displayed her slender and shapely figure to good advantage. She also came to the audition sporting a big red bouffant wig on her head. According to the *Internet Movie Database*, Sagal wanted Peg to be attired in 1960s-type garments "because she wanted to parody the 1960s housewife." The writers decided that Sagal's Peg was a winner and she got the part.

More than 300 actors auditioned for the part of Al Bundy. Among them was Michael Richards, who would catapult to fame in a couple of years for playing Kramer on *Seinfeld* (1989-1998) and much later plunge into infamy for a meltdown at the Comedy Club in which he repeatedly screamed vile racist epithets at African-Americans. Moye recalls that actors auditioning for Al Bundy tended to have similar—but wrong—interpretations of the character. "80% of the actors who auditioned read like Ralph Kramden [played by Jackie Gleason on the classic TV sitcom *The Honeymooners*]," Moye observes. "The other 20% read like Jack Nicholson in *The Shining*."

Casting Director Marc Hirschfeld had seen Ed O'Neill in a stage production of the classic John Steinbeck drama *Of Mice and Men* and been impressed by O'Neill's work in that play. O'Neill had played the simple-minded, tragically doomed Lenny. Hirschfield believed Lenny had some important things in common with Al and wanted O'Neill to read for Al. When O'Neill was suggested to Moye, the latter asked, "Who the hell is Ed O'Neill?" After learning that O'Neill's background had to that point been in drama, Moye was skeptical that O'Neill was well equipped for comedy.

On the day he was to audition, O'Neill had just come from a handball game and was covered in sweat. In auditioning for Al, Ed O'Neill was told to just walk through the door of the Bundy house. As he did so, he let his shoulders fall and let out a loud sigh. Moye's skepticism evaporated. "That was Al Bundy!" Moye knew. Hirschfield observed that O'Neill nailed the "defeat mode" central to Al.

O'Neill said that when he read for the part, he patterned his attitude after an uncle of his. The *Internet Movie Database* quotes O'Neill as stating, "When I read the pilot, it just reminded me of my Uncle Joe… just a self-deprecating kind of guy. He'd come home from work, and his wife would maybe say, 'I ran over the dog this morning in the driveway.' And he would say, 'Fine, what's for dinner?'" He also said that he later learned that most actors who auditioned for Al came off as angry (á la Ralph Kramden) while he tried to sound "resigned" like Uncle Joe which Leavitt and Moye knew was the right attitude for the part.

Perhaps O'Neill was aided by his working-class background as the son of a man who worked as a steelworker and truck driver and a woman who was a social worker.

As it turned out, O'Neill would enjoy the distinction of being the *only* performer to appear in all 206 episodes of *MWC*.

The writers created the part of the uptight neighbor Steve Rhoades specifically for actor David Garrison—who was in fact the very first actor cast for the show. Garrison had often played in stage productions. On TV, he had played Norman Lamb in the short-lived comedy series *It's Your Move*. Garrison was happy to play Steve.

Many actresses auditioned for the part of Steve's wife, Marcy Rhoades. Amanda Bearse seemed a natural fit when she read for Marcy, perfectly capturing Marcy's fresh-faced idealism. It is also probable that Bearse's previous acting experience prepared her well for the part of a best friend and confidant. On the popular soap opera *All My Children*, Bearse had played a character who shared her first name, Amanda Cousins, and who was the best friend of the conniving Liza Colby. Of course, Liza Colby was quite different from Peg Bundy as Liza came from a moneyed family and was portrayed as an insufferable snob. Nevertheless, playing Liza's pal may have been good preparation for playing Peg's pal. It was just as important, perhaps even more so, that Bearse be believable as Steve's wife. In an interview with this writer, Garrison recalled that when Bearse read with him, "It was clear from the read that the chemistry was there." Like the name Bundy, that of Rhoades was inspired by a wrestler, Dusty Rhodes.

The Bundy dog was a Briard named Buck. The large size of the breed coupled with its thick long hair, gave Buck a somewhat disheveled appearance that seemed in keeping with the program's ambience. Although Peg would once say of the dog, "he knows nothing," Buck was a highly intelligent dog who would prove quite easy to train.

The first season of the show had a character named Luke Ventura. Since Moye and Leavitt were wrestling fans, they named the character after the famous wrestler Jesse Ventura.

Comic and actor Ritch Shydner discussed how he was picked for this role in his book, *Kicking Through The Ashes—My Life As A Stand-up In The 1980s Boom*. He writes, "In the fall of 1986 I auditioned for a sitcom pilot, *Married With Children*. The role was 'Luke Ventura,' the single, womanizing co-worker of the show's lead."

Discussing the audition, Shydner elaborates, "I went to network for *Married With Children*, sitting with two other guys in a hallway on the Paramount lot. We all participated in the usual nervous chitchat. One of the actors just flew in from New York, his luggage next to him." Moye and Leavitt entered. Shydner continues, "The New York Actor sitting across from me jumped to his feet and shouted, 'Hey, Michael!'

"Michael Moye, one of the men about to decide the fate of this role, then embraced my

When someone from Research and Development suggested softening the Al Bundy character, the feisty Ron Leavitt retorted, "And you, sir, are why television sucks!"

Michael Moye, like *MWC* co-creator Ron Leavitt, often dressed casually but boasted solid TV sitcom writing credentials.

competition warmly. They joked and laughed before Michael told the guy, 'The wife has your room ready. You're going to love this town.'

"Leavitt and Moye then disappeared into the offices. The third actor looked like I felt, gut shot. I considered leaving, and then for some reason just started laughing at the whole damn affair."

When called into the office, Shydner writes, "For the first time ever I walked into an audition not worried about getting the part. I was loose and full of attitude, making fun of everything and everyone, including this alleged network, FOX, which didn't yet exist. I never got that many laughs in an audition, ever."

Two days after that audition, Shydner's agent, Bill Gross, told Shydner to prepare to tape the *MWC* pilot. However, everything did not go smoothly for Shydner. In his book, he recalls, "On the first day of rehearsal, Michael Moye pulled me aside and accused me of doing cocaine during the shooting of the pilot. He said I was 'acting coked up' and that someone found snow seals on a bathroom floor." Shydner answered that he might appear "whacked" because of nervousness, cigarettes, and soft drinks but insisted he was perfectly sober and clean of cocaine. He explains that the person who had left cocaine on the bathroom was discovered to be someone else but writes that Moye never apologized for the accusation. In fact, Shydner states Moye seemed to dislike Shydner, explaining, "he continued to hound me, hating everything I did, table readings, rehearsals, and the way I parked my car." However, this did not ruin his *MWC* experience. Shydner writes, "Fortunately, I had a lot of support from the other cast members. I can't tell you how much Ed O'Neill helped me with acting tips and pep talks." In an interview with this writer, Shydner sang O'Neill's praises, commenting, "Ed O'Neill was the best thing about working on that show."

THE STUMBLING BLOCK

As the show was being cast, a stumbling block to getting it on the air appeared. Moye wryly recalls, "I found out about this evil entity called Research and Development. I have a little bit of aversion to Research and Development based upon the fact that they are always wrong."

Leavitt and Moye sat in at a meeting of FOX executives. Officials from Research and Development displayed graphs and pie charts about reactions of people to suggestions about the potential program. One researcher stated that if Al Bundy would regularly hug his children either during an episode or at the end of it, the writers could get away with much of the outrageousness that they proposed. Moye remembers that a distinctly perturbed Leavitt stood up and told the researcher, "And you, sir, are why television sucks!"

The iconoclastic team of Moye and Leavitt wanted the freedom to create a show based on their specific vision and the Al Bundy they envisioned did not hug his kids unless they were bleeding. Ancier dismissed the Research and Development findings and convinced FOX officials to air the program as Moye and Leavitt wrote it.

However, before a pilot was aired, a pilot was filmed that was *not* aired. The first pilot film starred Tina Caspary as daughter Kelly and Hunter Carson as son Bud. Caspary and Carson were competent child actors but O'Neill believed the chemistry of the child actors was not quite right. Christina Applegate and David Faustino were cast as the Bundy kids. Both had acted since before they could form memories. At five months of age, Applegate made her debut in a commercial for disposable diapers. At only three months, Faustino played a baby daughter of Lily Tomlin on a TV special. O'Neill felt the chemistry was perfect with these child performers.

PILOT WITH A POW!

MARRIED... WITH CHILDREN, the first prime time series of the FOX Broadcasting Company, debuted on Sunday, April 5, 1987. The show began by displaying a fountain and then cars on an interstate while Frank Sinatra croons the classic song "Love and Marriage."

The fountain seen is Buckingham Fountain, a Chicago, Illinois landmark that is famously constructed in a rococo wedding cake style. That shot established Chicago as the setting for the program that would follow. The cars driving along the interstate are a shot from the 1983 comedy, *National Lampoon's Vacation*.

After the opening shots, the single word *Married* appears in letters in which paint appears to be dripping. Then the words *with Children* appear inside a rectangle resembling a license plate. The display of *with Children* is accompanied by a "clank" noise. A "slam" is heard before the program proper begins. We see the outside of a fairly ordinary house. (Although the story was clearly set in Chicago, the house that had its front displayed is in Deerfield, Illinois.) The peculiar opening seems to suggest a very different sort of program from what viewers had likely been used to and was wryly appropriate for *MWC*.

The camera moves indoors and the major characters of the show are introduced. The audience sees Al Bundy (Ed O'Neill) sitting on a couch in a drab, cheaply furnished, working-class living room. A middle-aged man in simple brown pants and an orange shirt, Al looks depressed and downtrodden as he hands cash to his pretty teenaged blonde daughter Kelly Bundy (Christina Applegate), then to his pre-teen son Bud Bundy (David Faustino), then to his good-looking and shapely red-haired wife Peg Bundy (Katey Sagal), and finally places cash in the mouth of a big dog with fluffy dark hair that we will come to know as Buck. The last cash placement was a sourly humorous comment on how this man, who is obviously cash-starved, feels financially squeezed by *everyone* around him.

The next scene shows Bud coming up behind Kelly and grabbing her hair.

Kelly shouts for him to leave her alone.

Holding his sister's hair and drawing a play knife across her throat, Bud enthusiastically shouts, "Die, commie bimbo!"

From the kitchen where Peg is clipping coupons, Peg remonstrates with her son for his teasing of his sister.

The kids head for school. Al walks down the stairs in a desultory manner. His hand is bandaged and he is holding a small potted plant. He says, "Sweetie, is this your little cactus?"

She tells him it is. The wounded man asks if there happened to be any special reason she placed it where the alarm clock had previously been.

Peg explains that it was an attempt to beautify the room and adds, "I meant to tell you to be careful before you slammed your hand into the alarm this morning."

"But you didn't," he pointedly notes—thus, the bandage.

Al looks in the refrigerator and gripes about the absence of juice. Peg admits she forgot to buy some and suggests he buy some on his way home from work.

The scene soon cuts to Al working in a shoe store. The set for the shoe store had previously been used as a travel agency set in *One Day at a Time*, a CBS sitcom broadcast from 1975-1984.

A CHILD (Victor DiMattia) is playfully brushing aside shoes and pounding them as his apparent mother, a large woman (Diana Bellamy) in a simple red dress, lifts a foot before Al for fitting. Annoyed, she asserts that despite what his ruler finds, her feet are size seven and have been all her adult life.

Al insists she is a nine and asks why she cannot just accept that fact.

She irritably exclaims that he is "very fresh!"

He tells her he can hardly be fresh after working with her feet for such a long time.

The two bitterly banter some more before the insulted woman grabs her son and leaves in a huff.

Then in walks fellow shoe salesman Luke Ventura (Ritch Shydner). With a devil-may-care demeanor, the broad-shouldered and blond-haired man asks if he can go to lunch.

Al replies that Luke just came from lunch.

The happy-go-lucky Luke readily acknowledges that this is "technically" true but reveals that he was actually having sex.

Luke is soon serving a Playboy-centerfold-worthy customer (Linda Dona) while Al attends to a mature and drably attired woman (Sue Ann Gilfillan).

Al is on his way to the back of the shoe store when Luke takes him aside. Luke says he has two tickets to a basketball game and asks if Al wants to accompany him. Al assures him that he does. When Luke wonders aloud if it will be OK with Al's wife, Al declares that he does not take orders from women.

The older woman in the chair orders him to get her shoes and he instantly obeys her order.

The scene cuts to Peg lying on the living room couch and watching TV. She hears the door start to open and instantly picks up the vacuum cleaner to make it look like she has been busy with housework. Al opens the door to find her industriously vacuuming.

Early in the conversation, Peg assures Al that she has been busy all day keeping the house clean. He seems to realize that her day has been more leisurely than she lets on. She soon admits she did not buy the juice he wanted her to buy.

Al informs Peg that he is going to the basketball game with Luke. Peg tells him he cannot attend the game because she has invited their new next-door neighbors, a "honeymoon couple," over to the house for the evening. Peg says she yearns for friends so he must be polite and cordial to the neighbors she has invited to the home. He tells her he is going to the game.

He is about to leave when Peg points out that both their credit cards and bank cards are in both their names—and the stores are open.

She has won. He realizes that he must stay.

The door opens and bright little Bud is home. He asks Dad for $5.

Dad Bundy pointedly wonders aloud if Bud has ever considered trying to earn his money. Bud asks if Al wants to know who Kelly was with that afternoon.

Al is eager to know the identity of his daughter's date.

Bud puts his hand out. Al puts the cash in the boy's hand and Bud gleefully spills the beans: "Cobra."

Conscientious Marcy often acted as a foil to conniving and lazy Peg.

Al learns that Bud is going to the basketball game his Dad must miss as Bud leaves the house.

Kelly comes downstairs. She wants Dad to give her some cash. Al coughs a few bucks up for his daughter and then asks who she spent her time with that afternoon.

She replies that she has not been with anyone.

Al brings up Cobra and she admits spending time with him. Kelly leaves on her date with the rather alarmingly nicknamed Cobra.

Steve Rhoades (David Garrison) and Marcy Rhoades (Amanda Bearse) knock on the door and are invited inside. With her dark brown hair and subdued attire consisting of a long skirt, white blouse, and pink sweater, Marcy gives an impression of primness. Steve appears brittle and restrained.

Marcy and Steve soon tell how they share most things, including housework. Of course, Marcy, unlike Peg, works outside the home. Nevertheless, Peg has a tone of "if-only-you would" when expressing admiration for Steve's housekeeping activities.

The couple reveals that Marcy has persuaded Steve to eschew sports viewings, as she believes it fosters unhealthy competition.

Marcy follows Peg into the Bundy kitchen. Marcy is perplexed by the odd way Peg is preparing coffee. Peg explains that she will make good coffee for herself and Marcy but makes lousy coffee for the men. She adds that the reason she serves awful coffee to the guys is so they will want to go out to eat at least occasionally.

Meanwhile, Al encourages Steve to watch sports despite Marcy's opposition. As Steve turns the TV on, Al thrusts his right hand down the front of his pants—a gesture that would become an Al Bundy trademark.

Peg and Marcy return to the living room. Marcy and Steve are soon having a spat about Steve's reawakened interest in sports. Still arguing, the couple leave.

Alone with his wife, Al asks if she would like to head upstairs—with the obvious implication that this trip is for marital lovemaking.

Peg wants exactly that. The episode ends with Al and Peg going upstairs and Al affectionately and lustily patting Peg's rump.

THE PILOT was a good introduction to the program and its major characters. Al is crude and downtrodden, Peg is conniving and a bit lazy, the kids are feisty, the dog is a big-haired lug, and neighbors Marcy and Steve appear dedicated to a political correctness that is all-too-ripe for some good-natured ribbing.

Some of the more salient aspects of the pilot were the way Al and Peg teased each other and the way both ridiculed other people. However, there was also a strong affection between Al and Peg. In that respect, the show appeared to *seriously* support the idea that love and marriage indeed "go together."

The pilot was also significant in the way it played with both liberal and conservative perceptions about marriage. Famous conservative Phyllis Schlafly would probably dislike *MWC* due to its habitual off-color jokes. However, in the scene in which Peg persuades Al to agree to her wishes because the bank and credit cards are in both their names "and the stores are still open," the program strongly supports an assertion Schlafly made: "Marriage is the best deal for women that the world has yet devised." In this scene, Peg dramatically yet comically demonstrates the power marriage can bestow upon a woman.

A FIRST SEASON SHOWCASES A SHOW'S FRESHNESS

The episodes that followed in *MWC*'s first season elaborated on many elements introduced in the pilot. Al is a man who is perennially dissatisfied, disliking his job selling women's shoes and feeling squeezed in by tight finances. Gerry Cohen has said, "Al Bundy was a man for whom life smelled bad." This emphasis on odor was also a trademark of the program as it frequently suggested that Al himself smelled bad and that he was especially troubled by his own bad foot odor as well as the foot odors of his shoe store customers.

Peg is an attractive middle-aged woman with a healthy sense of vanity who is also dissatisfied with her tight financial situation. She loves Al but is disappointed by his abilities as a breadwinner. As is typical of kids of their ages, Bud and Kelly often tease each other, sometimes light-heartedly and sometimes rather cruelly. Bud is intelligent and a bit of a "nerd." Kelly appears obsessed with attractiveness, popularity, and boyfriends. In one first season episode, she unashamedly calls herself a "boyfriend-stealer." Next-door neighbor Marcy Rhoades is a thin-skinned and high-strung feminist. Steven Rhoades is an uptight man who loves his wife and has strongly conflicting feelings toward Al, sometimes sympathizing with his traditionalist attitudes toward women and sometimes strongly backing his feminist wife.

The antagonism between Al and Marcy is established in the first season and milked for all it is worth. That first season also introduces the motif of Al razzing Marcy by comparing her to a chicken. There is an episode in which Marcy is at the Bundy house and a meal of salmon spills to the floor. When Al is asked if he sees a fish eye he responds, "No, but I do see a chicken leg."

Although *MWC* was definitely a groundbreaking sitcom, it could be seen in some respects as hearkening back to the equally groundbreaking *All in the Family*, another sitcom in which father did not always—or even usually—know best, and in which body functions and sexuality were frequent sources of humor. However, whereas that show's Archie Bunker was infamous for his all-around bigotry, Al Bundy appears to have nothing against blacks, Hispanics, Asians, Jews, and other groups. He may sometimes appear a champion male supremacist and show glimmers of homophobia but his one and only ethnic prejudice is an odd Franco-phobia. Al's dislike of the French is seen in Season 1. For example,

Jerry Hall as a sexy flight attendant with Al's co-worker Luke Ventura (Ritch Shydner). Photograph courtesy of Ritch Shydner.

he sees something written in French and, referring to World War II, says, "More people we should have killed." He makes a sarcastic reference to, "My friends the French." The first season also acquaints the audience with the show's ability to mine comedic gold from Al's tendency to insult customers at the shoe store. For example, a customer says, "I want something that goes with this dress." "A bubbling cauldron?" Al suggests.

The first season also established a pattern that would be followed throughout the series of giving episode names that recall other popular media. "Peggy Sue Got Work" is a clear reference to the 1986 comedy-drama *Peggy Sue Got Married*. "Nightmare on Al's Street" is a play on the famous horror film *A Nightmare On Elm Street*. Finally, "Johnny Be Gone" is a wonderful pun on the classic Chuck Berry rock tune "Johnny Be Good."

What's going on at the shoe store, Al?

Shydner states, "The seventh show featured my character [in a larger way than other episodes]. Al Bundy, after a terrible fight with his wife, Peg, came to stay at Luke's bachelor pad. Al flew from the temptation of the two blond flight attendants offered by Luke, later bringing home a blond wig for Peg to wear. During the taping, I waited behind the wall of my bedroom with one of the flight attendants, actress Jerry Hall. She was a beautiful woman with a cute Texas drawl, cracking me up with stories of her 'cheap' husband, Mick Jagger. I thought to myself, 'I can do this job.'"

However, Shydner told this author that playing Luke had its challenges. "Luke was an out and out womanizer," Shydner observes. "It took a bit to get free and loose with that, but I was getting it."

Nevertheless, Luke Ventura was written out after Episode 7 of Season 1. Shydner remembers, "The next Friday I didn't get a script. Bill Gross said not to worry; it was probably just a delivery problem. A few minutes later he called back with the news that I was no longer on the show. That's a firing, Hollywood-style."

It would be quite awhile later that Shydner learned the reason behind his character's finish. Ron Leavitt said, "Look, man. I'm sorry, but Michael

Actor Ritch Shydner played Al Bundy's promiscuous co-worker Luke Ventura in Season 1. Photograph courtesy of Ritch Shydner.

wanted that role for his friend. You wouldn't believe the scene in the office the day you auditioned. Michael fought like crazy but the network insisted on you. After that, Michael wanted to get rid of the role, and you. We were fighting so many fires I finally let him have his way."

There were two significant ways in which the first season of the program differed from the ten that would follow. Season 1 was the only season in which it is suggested that Al and Peg, after sixteen years of marriage, are still sexually intimate on a regular basis, and that Al usually initiates their lovemaking.

So what did you do this time, Al?

The first *MWC* season is also the only season in which housewife Peg is depicted as regularly performing housework. She is seen fixing and serving meals as well as carrying a basket of laundry. However, even in this season, we know that Peg is not an effective and efficient June Cleaver-style housewife. In the pilot, we see her relaxing on the couch to enjoy TV—only picking up the vacuum cleaner when she knows her husband is about to enter the house.

Perhaps the most important part of her being a housewife is that Peg *likes* being a housewife. "Peggy Sue Got Work" underlines this point. In this respect, the show skewered one of the primary pieties of feminist extremism that views "housewife" as a uniquely "oppressive" occupation. Marcy represents this sort of thinking when she insists that Peg will be much better off at a job. However, as Arianna Huffington rightly pointed out in her first book, *The Female Woman*, "women's libbers" tended to have a "lop-sided" view of the merits of paid work because they were often artists, academics, journalists, and the like. Faced with a choice between being a housewife and a more ordinary job, it is hardly irrational to prefer the former as Peg does. She yearns to watch *Oprah* and *Dr. Phil* and she finds those television programs, with their varied guests and multitude of matters discussed, far more interesting than ringing up orders in a store. Moreover, the workplace may include chores *identical* to those typically performed by a housewife, a fact underlined when we first see Peg behind the counter and cleaning that counter and its register with a feather duster. Standing behind the counter quickly becomes tiresome and she wants to be back home where she can take breaks as she sees fit and lie on the couch when she wishes. All of these things point to valid reasons why at least some women prefer to rely on a husband for support rather than earning money themselves.

Bundy family members are often seen going upstairs and coming downstairs. On a television documentary entitled *MTV's Backstage with the Bundys*, David Faustino revealed that "upstairs" did not include three bedrooms but only a little alcove. He added that the bored actors sometimes wrote on the walls of the "upstairs."

The first season, like the second, was taped at the ABC Television Center in Hollywood, California. This studio boasts a significant history in the entertainment world as portions of that seminal motion picture, *The Jazz Singer*, the first of the "talkies," were taped there. ABC has since moved out of what is now called Prospect Studios.

A CAST AND CREW STARTING OUT

DURING THE FIRST SEASON, the *MWC* viewing audience was small. Ancier observes, "Hardly any comedy show starts strong.... Until you understand the relationship between Al and Peg, you won't laugh."

Nevertheless, the unusual sitcom attracted the attention of critics and created a certain amount of buzz. It soon had a loyal, albeit small, group of regular watchers. Journalist Howard Polskin, who had once been a staff writer for *TV Guide*, comments, "It was the talk of water coolers."

One person who never expected the show to be a hit was O'Neill who said he thought it likely *MWC* would be canceled after its first six episodes. However, the program was destined to catapult him to fame. O'Neill first realized he was gaining fame when in a pizzeria. A teenaged boy did a double take on seeing the actor, then grinned and shoved a hand down the front of his pants in imitation of Al Bundy. "You start to realize that anonymity is a big thing to give up," O'Neill observed. By contrast, Katey Sagal was rarely recognized in public even when the show reached its peak of popularity. This is because she did not wear the Peg Bundy wig in private life and people strongly associated Peg with the bubble of bright red hair. David Faustino recalled being at a crowded mall during its first season, wearing a shirt that had the show's logo on it. No one said anything to him about performing as Bud Bundy or appeared to recognize him.

David Garrison recalled that the most challenging aspect of depicting Steve Rhoades was "keeping a balance between nerdy and nifty. There was always the possibility and hope that given half a chance, Steve could cut loose." The biggest challenge of regularly acting on the show for Garrison was "developing a talent for short-term memorization. Not only do actors on series learn a new script each week, but also scripts often change during the week, and sometimes even during show tapings."

Al with Buck, the big hairy dog who added so much, in both humor and warmth, to the program.

Memorization also provided a challenge for the four-legged star of the program, dog trainer Steve Ritt states. "It is hard for any dog to be able to do a live show because sometimes he would have to enter the scene after nine or fifteen pages of dialogue to perform, so he would have to remember what he was supposed to do through a long lapse of time," Ritt comments. "That is hard for any dog even though I was guiding him with hand signals. You can't *just* rely on hand signals because with live shows the dog has to be just on the right beat, not a second earlier or a second later, or the joke doesn't work."

On at least one occasion, affection between *MWC* actors caused a problem. "Buck loved Ed O'Neill and during one taping Buck all of a sudden started kissing Ed on the face in the middle of a scene so Ed was unable to deliver his lines," Ritt recalls.

About playing Luke Ventura, Shydner writes, "My role was small but in every episode. I worked hard and got into a groove. On Friday, the script was delivered. I worked lines with an acting coach over the weekend, and scored the expected laughs at the table read on Monday. My confidence was growing. I was starting to have fun and get loose."

Scott I. Glickman was one of two boom operators on *MWC*. He explains, "For anyone who doesn't know what a boom is, it's an apparatus that you stand on or sit on in order to operate the microphone that is on the end of it. The boom has a long arm that can go as far as 26 feet out and at the end is a microphone that picks up all the dialogue or any sounds like a door knocking that we need to record." Glickman and the other boom operator, Alan Zema, worked with the sound mixer to choreograph *MWC*. "We would stand and watch with our scripts open and we marked the scripts as to who to which boom operator is supposed to boom that dialogue or those sounds," Glickman elaborates. "For example, say Katey Sagal and David Faustino were sitting at the kitchen table. I might boom the two of them at the table. If Katey got up and walked into the living room where Al was but she and Al were split apart for a way, I might boom Peg and Alan might boom Al."

The successful comedy of the show sometimes made Glickman's job difficult: "One challenge was not to let myself get laughing so hard that I couldn't even see what I was doing. The show was so funny that I would sometimes get tears in my eyes because I was laughing so hard."

There was a wonderful sense of warmth among cast and crew, Glickman relates. "I've been doing sitcoms since the middle 1970s. I worked on shows like *All in the Family* and *The Jeffersons*. *Married… With Children* had one of the nicest casts I ever knew and one of the funniest writing staffs."

When asked if he ever found any fellow cast members difficult, David Garrison answered, "We were all having too much fun to have difficulties." He recalled his fellow *MWC* cast members with genuine warmth. "Of course, I have a special fondness for Amanda Bearse, as we were scene partners more often than not, and she is a delight both onstage and off, but we all worked well together."

SHAKING IT UP WITH SECOND AND THIRD SEASONS

MWC GOT ITS SECOND SEASON up to a rousing and rollicking start with a two-part episode entitled "Poppy's by the Tree." With this sprightly episode the show more than lived up to its envelope-pushing reputation as it aired an episode that brilliantly spoofed such institutions as family vacations, small towns, celebrity—and spoofed serial murderers!

The first episode begins with scenes showing us that a small Florida town's hotel has been plagued by a serial murderer who axes tourists to death every few years. He is expected to murder again in 1987—the year the Bundy family vacations in the appropriately named Dumpwater, Florida. When the Bundys arrive, they soon learn that one of Dumpwater's chief attractions is a citizen who gives speeches about having once met a celebrity. This citizen is "The Man Who Met Andy Griffith." The mention of this is a sly way of underlining the difference between *MWC*, on its way to becoming a TV classic due to its raunchy content, and the wholesome classic sitcom *The Andy Griffith Show*. Indeed, *MWC* would make a regular practice of mining comedic gold by making fun of other TV shows. The first episode of "Poppy's" has a cliffhanger ending with Peg and Al screaming when a huge knife suddenly cuts through their bed!

Episode 2 of "Poppy's by the Tree" starts with the family running from the axe murderer. They run downstairs to the hotel lobby. The sheriff shows up and informs the Bundys that there is a serial murderer in Dumpwater who targets tourists—and that the rain has washed out the bridge. The sheriff's desultory lack of concern is wonderfully comic. After he leaves to return to bed, the panicked Bundys are left to defend themselves. The Bundys return to their hotel suite. Al finds a man (Gary Grubbs) lurking in a closet, overpowers him, and drags him to the crowded hotel lobby—where both are ignored. The sheriff appears. "He's the killer!" Al shouts. The sheriff, sounding both exasperated and dismayed, says, "But that's

Peg's poor homemaking meant that Al sometimes could not find a matching pair of (however smelly) socks.

Delbert." He contends that Delbert is no murderer but "a klepto"—and the deputy! The sheriff assures Al that he should not worry about the axe murderer since he and Delbert are investigating.

Grubbs recalls being perplexed when his agent advised him to audition for the part of Delbert. "I'd been doing shows for ABC, NBC, and CBS," he explains. "What was FOX? It was a network that was just starting out. I'd never even heard of the show *Married with Children*! But my agent told me the pay was the same so I decided to do it. We did a table read and I saw how funny everyone was." Grubbs was very happy to get cast as Delbert. "I had a great time doing it. We had a lot of freedom. They'd let you add a line if you wanted to."

Grubbs found that he very much enjoyed playing the odd combination of kleptomaniac and deputy. "It was fun for me," Grubbs states, "because I was playing a creepy character and they allowed me the freedom to make Delbert a *likeable* creep and that's what I wanted to do!" How does

From Season 2 on, lack of sexual intimacy in the Bundy marriage because a regular motif.

a performer make a "creep" likeable? "That's actor craft. It is not taking yourself too seriously. I made Delbert just a little slow on the uptake and a little weird but there was no meanness about him. My niche might be playing the likeable creep. You do that by not making a mean face and keeping your voice high instead of low."

When Al tells the kids they are leaving Dumpwater, Kelly indicates they are missing something—Mom! We then see that Peg has been tied up by a peculiarly smooth-talking maniac. Al finds Peg and manages to overpower this serial murderer. The sheriff and some townspeople rush into the room. They see who the murderer is—and do not arrest him. The sheriff asks, "Do you know who this is?" Al answers that he is the serial murderer who has terrorized the town's tourists for years. "But he's also The Man Who Met Andy Griffith," someone says. Then it is explained: "Dumpwater ain't much of a town. All we've got is a serial killer and The Man Who Met Andy Griffith. We could afford to lose one but we're damned if we're going to lose both." The episode ends with the baffled Bundys returning to Chicago.

The first *MWC* episode with a Christmas storyline was a Season 2 episode entitled "You Better Watch Out." When asked, "What was the funniest thing that ever happened to you while playing Steve Rhoades?" David Garrison answered, "All of us trying to keep our composure on camera during the first Christmas episode when Santa's parachute failed to deploy, and he crashed into the Bundy's backyard. If you watch the episode carefully, you can see that the director cuts away just as we were all about to lose it on set."

Season 2 introduced several special tropes that would become trademarks of the show. During this season, Kelly's character—previously a girl of seemingly normal intelligence—became a "dumb blonde." Her mental denseness served as comic fodder throughout the rest of *MWC*. This second season included the introduction of the "Bundy Cheer," in which Al would lead the

As might be expected, a camping trip on MWC has complications

Ian Patrick Williams as cook Beany and Gary Grubbs as kleptomaniac/Deputy Delbert. Credit to Gary Grubbs for photograph.

entire family in exclaiming, "Whoa, Bundy!" This season also introduced a voiceover for Buck the dog.

An interesting aspect of the episode entitled "All In The Family" is that King Kong Bundy, the inspiration for the Bundy family name, guest stars. He plays Peg's Uncle Irwin Wanker (Peg's last name was Wanker before it became Bundy). This was the first of two *MWC* episodes in which King Kong Bundy appeared.

THE PLACE AT WHICH *MWC* was taped would change for Season 3. It was still in Hollywood but at Stage 9 of Sunset-Gower Studios. This is where *MWC* would continue to be taped through Season 8.

The early part of the third season boasted highly creative episodes such as "Sweatland" in which Peg and others believe Al sweated an image of Elvis Presley on a shirt.

However, the most powerful—and oddly poignant—early episode of Season 3 was "He Thought He Could," about a comically nightmarish situation caused by a decades-overdue library book. Al finds a copy of

The Little Engine That Could—which he checked out of a library in 1957! Thus, the entire plot device for this episode revolves around what must be a common fear: the long forgotten and extraordinarily overdue library

Ahhhh… Peg snoozes after relishing a delivered pizza

book that has accumulated a monstrously large fine. Right after Al finds the overdue book, a flashback is shown. Little Al Bundy, played by Edan Gross and shown with his right hand down the front of his pants, confronts an auburn-haired, heavyset librarian named Miss DeGroot (Lu Leonard). Glaring at Al, she declares, "Young Mr. Bundy—the devil boy." When he checks out *The Little Engine*, she ominously warns, "I'll be waiting for you." The flashback ends. Al expresses trepidation about seeing Miss DeGroot again. "That was thirty years ago—the woman's probably dead," Steve observes. Reassured by his friend's observation, Al decides to return the book. However, when he goes to the library, he sees that Miss DeGroot is very much alive and still the librarian. Now silver-haired, she recognizes Al and tells him he owes over $2,000 for *The Little Engine*. He fibs that he returned the book many years ago. Distracting her by pushing a ladder, he slips the volume into the stacks. Then he points to it and says it was there all along. When he returns home he learns from the TV that library surveillance cameras caught him sliding the book onto the shelf. Vowing to pay the horrible fine, Al once again returns to the library. Al has his final confrontation with Miss DeGroot who reviles him as a "total and complete loser."

Al retorts, "So you think I'm a loser? Just because I've got a stinking job that I hate, a family that doesn't respect me, and a whole city that curses the day I was born?" After noting all the things his life lacks, and admitting he will "never be what I wanted to be," he stoutly affirms his will to live: "The fact that I haven't put a gun in my mouth, you pudding of a woman, makes me a winner!" The soliloquy is both funny and oddly poignant, making it an example of *MWC* at its best. At the episode's end, Al does not make an arrangement to pay the fine, but instead steals Miss

DeGroot's little bowl of sugar—perhaps to fulfill a childhood threat to pour the bowl's contents in her car's gas tank.

Perhaps the most important episode in Season 3, and indeed, one of the most important *MWC* episodes ever, was the sixth episode of the third season because it would lead to complications for the program that would put it in jeopardy but also help make it a great hit.

UNWANTED PUBLICITY BOOST: TERRY RAKOLTA

Although *MWC* had its hardy band of loyal fans, it was not doing terribly well in the ratings by the time Episode 6 of Season 3 aired. Moye comments, "Every week it built and built." However, FOX did not believe the audience was building fast enough and was considering canceling the sitcom. The show might very well have not seen a fourth season but for a very unexpected—and initially unwanted—publicity boost.

The roots of that boost were laid when a slender, blonde, and strikingly attractive Bloomfield Hills, Michigan housewife named Terry Rakolta sat down with her three children in her home to watch a TV show she had never before seen.

Rakolta's husband was John Rakolta, CEO of Walbridge. Her sister, Ronna Romney, was married to G. Scott Romney, son of former Michigan Governor and Presidential candidate George Romney and brother of former Massachusetts Governor and Presidential candidate Mitt Romney.

Terry Rakolta knew nothing about the program but assumed from its title, *Married... with Children,* together with the fact that it started at 8:30 p.m., that it was appropriate family programming.

The episode Rakolta and her kids watched on January 15, 1989 was entitled "Her Cups Runneth Over." The episode begins with Peg dancing and lip-synching to Aretha Franklin singing "R-E-S-P-E-C-T." Bud and Kelly watch from the stairs. Bud comments that the two of them watch their Mom do the same thing every year. "The birthday hop." They predict accurately that Peg will get depressed when she realizes she is another year older. Al arrives. Peg complains about her aging and how she yearns for something for her birthday. She wails, "The best years of my life are gone—and the worst part is, I spent them with you!" She demands cash to shop to cheer herself up. Al forks over the money and she reminds him, "This doesn't get you out of getting me a present."

Peg returns from a shopping spree laden down with two full shopping bags but still depressed. She has learned of a new catastrophe: "They discontinued my bra! My Fancy Figure 327 is a thing of the past!"

Steve comes over for a visit. He informs Al that there is a store in Wisconsin called Francine's that specializes in sexy women's lingerie and might have the Fancy Figure 327. To placate Peg, Al agrees to drive to Wisconsin.

We cut to a scene of Al and Steve in Francine's. Both ogle the shapely young ladies who patronize and work at the store. A leather-clad mannequin intrigues Steve who gingerly touches an artificial nipple covered by a black leather pasty. Al spots a fellow with a tiara on his head gazing into a handheld mirror. Al remarks, "And they wonder why we call them queens!"

Al gets into a conversation with an older male store clerk (Bill Smillie) who is seated behind a counter and wearing an ordinary man's shirt. A woman tells the clerk that his wife has called. When he walks out from the counter we see that in addition to the shirt he is wearing stockings, a garter belt, and high heels.

A lovely brown-haired woman (Devin DeVasquez) in a dressing room calls out to Al: "If you were my boyfriend, would you like this?" She lets the drapes fall and Al sees her in a bra, panties, garter, and stockings. He is clearly aroused. She asks, "What about without the bra?" The audience only sees her from behind as she appears to display her breasts to Al—who faints. As well he might: the sensuous and shapely DeVasquez had been *Playboy* magazine's Miss June 1985.

We return to the Bundy house. Peg answers the door. A young male cop (Deron McBee) is there. He threatens to arrest Peg for traffic tickets. She appears confused and asks if there is a way to work this out. "We can dance!" he shouts as he tears off his cop uniform, revealing himself to be a male stripper. "Happy birthday!" Marcy exclaims.

The show ends with Al coming home to Peg. Al brings Peg the bra she craves. What's more, he has ten of them! The episode appears to end on a note of warmth. But just as it is about to go off the air, Al inquires, "Peg, who's the cop with his pants on backwards?"

Rakolta was outraged by the episode. She recalls, "I sent my three children out of the room after five minutes of this trash." However, she continued to watch in order to take down the names of the companies advertising on the program. Rakolta has always maintained "I am not a prude" but she thought much of the show just went too far. Her major complaints were about Steve touching the nipples of the leather-clad mannequin, the elderly gentleman garbed in stockings and a garter belt, the woman taking off her bra in front of Al (although her breasts are not shown to the TV audience), and the apparently gay man wearing a tiara with Al commenting, "And they wonder why we call them 'queens.'"

Believing *MWC* was unacceptably vulgar, Rakolta resolved to do something about the show. Having taken down the names of the companies advertising on it, she fired off letters to them, demanding they drop their sponsorship. Talk shows began regularly interviewing her. It may be mildly ironic but a factor in her making the talk show rounds might have been her good grooming and attractive appearance. The crusader against too much sex on television possessed considerable sex appeal.

Michael Moye recalled being nonplussed when he first heard about Rakolta's objections. Moye said, "They said a housewife objected. As in *one* housewife!" Moye held up an index finger and incredulously asked, "And I was supposed to take this seriously?"

FOX acknowledged that Tambrands, makers of Tampax, stopped advertising with *MWC*. Rakolta pointed to two other companies as also dropping ads with the show. One was McNeil Consumer Products Co. for their Medipren. The company's President wrote to Rakolta that the ad had been "purchased as an oversight." The other business was Sandoz/Dorsey Inc., makers of Triaminic Nite Lite.

Other companies responded to Rakolta in ways that suggested they sympathized with her concerns—but then continued advertising with *MWC* despite those letters. Coca-Cola President Ira Herbert sent an epistle to Rakolta in which he wrote: "I am corporately, professionally, and personally embarrassed that one of our commercials appeared in this particularly unsuitable program episode." Mitsubishi Motor Sales of America Advertising Manager Frances Oda also wrote to Rakolta, stating that the business had "no plans" to continue advertising with *MWC*.

Nevertheless, both Coca-Cola and Mitsubishi had further ads appearing on *MWC*.

FOX changed the time the show aired from 8:30 p.m. to 9:00 p.m. That half hour change, while certainly a small step, was probably a good thing. It is true that children would be less likely to tune in at 9:00 p.m. than at 8:30 p.m. It is also true that parts of *MWC* were simply inappropriate for youngsters. Although many derided Rakolta as the prude she said she was not, she did have a point regarding the suitability of the show for kids. Moreover, that time change may have contributed to continued advertising by companies such as Coca-Cola and Mitsubishi. Indeed, Oda cited the little time change as making "a big difference."

As a result of Rakolta's campaign, FOX decided against airing an episode that had been filmed entitled "I'll See You in Court" because it was considered quite raunchy. The episode became known as the "Lost Episode." In the United States, it premiered thirteen years after it was filmed. The first American airing was on June 18, 2002 on FX, the FOX re-run channel.

Rakolta's campaign against the show piqued the curiosity of many people who wanted to know what all the fuss was about. When asked what he believed was the oddest incident that occurred while he played Steve Rhoades, David Garrison answered, "Probably the whole controversy about one Michigan viewer's attempt to get sponsors to quit the show. Of course, her strategy backfired, only making the show that much more popular."

Indeed, the show's ratings soared as Rakolta worked against it. Many of the curious viewers became fans of the show. It is likely that her campaign may have been partially responsible for the longevity of the program.

The key word here is "partially." Although many people undoubtedly tuned in because of her campaign, it is a certainty that the program would not have acquired new fans if it had not had much to offer. People *continued* watching because the show was very funny and its deeply flawed characters believable and endearing.

As Christina Applegate notes, "The show definitely shocked and disgusted people. But, privately, they enjoyed laughing at it. I think all too often people look at the perfect families on television and think, 'Why can't my family be like that?' In the case of *Married... with Children*, people were able to say, 'Thank God my family's not like that!'"

Ed O'Neill recalls that playing Al Bundy "helped put me on the map." However, it also had a downside: "It was like being known for being Porky Pig."

SEASON 4: GRILLS, CHILLS, AND DOGGY THRILLS

DAVID GARRISON REMARKED that what he enjoyed most about being part of *MWC* was "breaking the rules of the family sitcom form. It was the first show of its kind, and it turned the half-hour family comedy on its head, paving the way for many others including, for instance, *The Simpsons*. It was the first time father didn't know best, and it's always fun to break the rules."

The fourth season continued gleefully and creatively breaking the traditional sitcom rules—and having loads of fun doing it. Season 4 started off with "Hot Off The Grill," an episode truly gross. Al hosts a backyard barbecue for Labor Day. The usual roles are reversed when Al induces Peg to vigorously scrub away at a table. The sight of her working gets Al horny and he repeatedly whisks her away for sex. When the grilling proper is done, Steve compliments Al on the hamburgers. Al says his secret is to never change the ashes. Marcy says the talk about ashes reminds her of her poor aunt whose ashes are in an urn. Overhearing this, Kelly is shocked and sickened: she realizes those ashes were put in the grill!

Episode 3 is entitled "Buck Saves the Day" and is significant for the amount and variety of work required of the canine actor. Boom operator Scott I. Glickman told this writer, "Buck was just the most amazing animal I've come across." However, the story of the episode belies the title. Al, Bud, Steve, and

The housewife visiting the breadwinner at his place of business

Bundy siblings share a giggle

a group of kids end up stranded in the forest. Al has a brainstorm: the women will rescue them. He will send Buck home with a note in his mouth! Al puts the note between the dog's lips and Buck is on his way. We see the energetic Buck running through the forest, jumping over a log, and then wading through a stream. However, when he gets to the Bundy home, Buck runs inside and takes a place on the couch. He growls rather than show the note in his mouth. The episode ends with the guys miserable in the forest and Buck comfortably snoozing on the couch.

Episode 5 is entitled "He Ain't Much, But He's Mine" and, like many of the best *MWC* episodes, combines humor with poignancy. Peg suspects Al is cheating on her with a woman she knows from the beauty parlor. Of course, this turns out to be unfounded. This episode, like several others, underlined basic truths about the Bundy marriage. However full of disappointment, there was love between Al and Peg. What's more, each was always faithful to the other.

Episode 7 was particularly interesting in the *MWC* canon and a harbinger of even more interesting things to come. In "Desperately Seeking Miss October," *MWC* branches out from its usual reality-based comedy to embrace comedy based on sheer fantasy. Indeed, the episode could be considered horror-comedy as a ghost—yes, a ghost—makes an appearance in "Desperately Seeking Miss October." The story starts with Peg hearing about a woman who won the lottery after rubbing the belly of a good luck sculpture called a "Toobroo." She buys that item—selling a collection of *Playboys* that Al inherited from his Dad to do so. At the shoe store, Steve visits Al. The two men soon compete for the attention of a lovely young woman who has come into the store. They recognize her as Brandi Brandt (playing herself), *Playboy's* Miss October 1987. When Al returns home, he dashes downstairs to the basement to look her up in his collection of *Playboys*—only to discover the collection is gone. Peg confesses that she sold the collection and then tries to soothe him by suggesting he rub Toobroo's belly. When he is alone, Al sits on the couch mourning the loss of his beloved *Playboy* collection. A toilet is heard flushing. Out comes an older version of Al with graying hair and a thick gray mustache. We soon learn it is the ghost of his Dad. (Do ghosts urinate and defecate? Do Heaven and Hades need toilets?) Dad asks after the kids and Al glumly answers that they are fine. Then Dad asks about his *Playboys*. Al realizes he knows of the terrible loss. Dad is disappointed in Al but goes on to give Al a pep talk, saying John Wayne in heaven is betting that Al can get the treasures back.

Soon, Al orders Peg to retrieve the *Playboys*. A scene follows in which she comes into the house with a wheelbarrow filled with the collection. The episode ends with Al taking an enthusiastic Peg upstairs for some *Playboy*-inspired sex.

Episode 8 might be viewed as a kind of sardonic comment on the pitfalls of misdirected entrepreneurship. It is entitled "967-SHOE." The episode begins with Al realizing that his credit cards have been canceled. Then he goes through the bills. He cries out in pain, putting his face in his hands. He has a sudden brainstorm: people call to talk about sex and to talk to psychics, so people should want to call a toll phone line to get advice about shoes! The scene switches to Steve. He is at the bank, making loans like crazy because there is a contest in which the banker who makes the most loans wins a free trip to Hawaii. Al comes in and asks for a loan for his projected toll shoe advice phone line. Steve tells him no banker would even consider a loan for such a crackpot idea. Then another banker goes to the board and puts on that he got another loan that puts him in the lead for the free visit to the Aloha State. Steve immediately gives Al the loan and wins the trip! Needless to say, the "Dr. Shoe" line is a money-losing flop. The episode ends with Steve fired, Marcy demoted to teller, and Al having mortgaged the Bundy residence for a period of over a hundred years.

On December 17, 1989, an episode made in two parts was broadcast as one hour-long episode. Entitled "It's A Bundyful Life," it is a wickedly witty take-off on the beloved Jimmy Stewart classic *It's A Wonderful Life*. Al announces to the family that this year he has the money for presents. It is good news since, as Kelly observes, Christmas without presents is like Thanksgiving without pizza. Thus, family members try to butter Al up so they will receive his largess. However, he cannot get to the bank to get the money. He makes futile attempts to raise the money. Ultimately, he must go home to tell the family the disappointing news. He has failed yet again. Peg has eight dollars so she and the kids go to Denny's for Christmas while Al starves at home. Alone at Christmas, Al tries to turn on the Christmas lights but only one puny light will actually light. It seems symbolic of his life of failure. He conks out in the snow. Then he is awakened by his guardian angel. Ironically, and perhaps meaningfully, his guardian angel is played by Sam Kinison—the actor for whom the part of Al Bundy was originally created. This overweight and slovenly guardian angel demonstrates his powers by making all the Christmas lights actually light. Then they go into the house to see what life would have been like had Al Bundy never been born. He finds Peg a prim and dutiful housewife, her hair up in a bun, and conscientiously fixing dinner. He finds "Budrick" well mannered and respectful of the female sex. He finds Kelly a virgin intellectual in college. Peg is the wife of, and the kids are the children of, a successful and genteel man named Jablonski played by Ted McGinley (who would one day become a vital regular on *MWC*). The guardian angel is dismayed. He has *not* shown Al Bundy a reason he should have been born! The angel will not be able to get his wings!

But Al Bundy declares that he cannot allow them to enjoy all that wholesome happiness after they have caused him so much misery. He wants to live to have his family be its rightfully dysfunctional self. The episode ends with Al assuring himself that Bud is crude, Kelly is stupid, and Peg is lazy. He is overjoyed because his true family has been returned to him. The angel is shocked but ecstatically pleased. Truly, this was a joyous and original tribute to a "Bundyful" life.

One of the most significant things that happened in the storyline of Season 4 occurred in an episode that first aired on February 11, 1990: To pursue his dream of being a forest ranger, Steve leaves Marcy. This was written into the script because David Garrison wanted to stop doing weekly television work and return to acting in live theater. The first actor cast in the series, he was the only regular cast member to leave the series. Marcy remains single for the rest of the season. Season 4 was also the first season in which the live audience started regularly applauding, and often whistling and hooting, when a major character entered a scene. This was also the time when some episodes branched out from reality-based comedy into speculative-based comedy.

As the Bundy kids grew, so did the actors who played them. Faustino and Applegate spent their teen years becoming famous and affluent. Applegate, at least, insists the experience did not make her into a spoiled brat. "I wasn't one to go out and buy a new car and stereo system and expensive clothes," she recalls. "My Mom helped keep me grounded."

SEASON 5: LOOK ALIVE AND THRIVE!

THE BUNDY FAMILY BECAME FAMOUS for how frequently they insulted each other. However, they typically got upset if someone outside the family did the same. In Episode 1 of Season 5, "We'll Follow the Sun," Al and another man quarrel. The man's wife inquires of him, "Don't you have anything better to do than pick a fight with a moron?" When Peg asks whom she is calling a "moron," the other woman replies, "Your husband, you painted hus—" She cannot complete the sentence because Peg starts beating the woman.

Perhaps the most notable aspect of Season 5's Episode 2, "Al... with Kelly" is the fantasy Al has of two women fighting over him, one of whom is played by the famously gorgeous Pamela Anderson.

One of the more inspired episodes of Season 5 was Episode 5, "Dance Show." It begins with Peg and Marcy visiting a dance club. Peg soon has a regular dance partner, a handsome fellow named Andy (Sam McMurray). Sitting home alone, Al hears a knock at the door. When Al opens the door, he sees Pete (Dan Castallenata, best known for voicing Homer in *The Simpsons*) who says, "Your wife has been seeing my husband." Al invites Pete in. The two chat and Al learns that Pete regularly cooks for Andy, has a job, and enjoys sports. "I love you," Al says. Pete ends up fixing a meal for Al. The ever-hungry Al gobbles greedily at the steak. Pete also brings a cake and apologizes for using the dog dish but points out that the Bundy kitchen lacks plates. Al eventually shows up at the dance club and remonstrates with Andy, telling him to go back to the good man who waits for him at home.

MWC had previously departed from its usual reality-based scenarios with the appearance of the ghost of Al's Dad and with the angel in "It's A Bundyful Life." It forayed into a whimsical science fiction based scenario with Season 5's Episode 7: "Married... with Aliens."

Peg enjoys a telephone chat

Al bangs his head. Then little green beings arrive and steal his socks. People assume that the injury to his head has caused hallucinations. The aliens go away when anyone else looks their way. However, Al gets a series of photographs of himself posed with the intergalactic travelers. He takes the photos to be developed, happily looking forward to life as a billionaire after he becomes the first man to prove the existence of extra-terrestrial life. Wouldn't you know it? As Bundy's luck would have it, the developing room has a problem and the pictures are destroyed. However, the audience is informed at the end that Al has done an enormous service for these inter-planetary travelers as they are using his smelly socks to get fuel for their space travels. Yes, that is what we are told by closing titles that read as follows: "Long ago, in the Galaxy Euryops, a great, menacing comet was born. Colossal in size, deadly in trajectory, it hurtled unstoppable through the Universe, on a collision course with many inhabited planets. Among the doomed was a small green world called Earth. But on planet Philydion they still sing songs of the man who made it possible for the comet to be destroyed. The man who saved Earth and a hundred worlds, by providing fuel for the ships which diverted the comet. And that man is… AL BUNDY."

The most important Season 5 episode for the series as a whole was Episode 12 ("Married… With Who") that saw Marcy depart her divorced status for a second marriage.

Marcy attends a banker's convention and gets drunk. She wakes up married to Jefferson D'Arcy (played by the same Ted McGinley who played Mr. Jablonski in the world as presented by Al's guardian angel and would have wed a June Cleaver-style Peg had Al never been born). Al learns Jefferson has been a con artist and moocher in his past; Peg agrees to give a "real" wedding to the already-married couple. As might be expected on this show, nothing goes right at that wedding in the Bundys' backyard.

One of the wildest episodes of the season saw Al's—very brief—ascent into becoming a man of power. In episode 13 ("The Godfather") Kelly dates alderman Harry Ashland (Lane Davies). Through Ashland, Al gains power and it quickly goes to his head. Al appears in a kind of "Godfather" costume, lowering his voice to sound like Marlon Brando as Don Corleone, and Jefferson and Marcy D'Arcy come to the house to grovel before him, even kissing his ring as Peg gleefully photographs the scene. One Bundy feels left out: Bud. Peg notes, "You're both our children. It's just that Kelly is now our favorite." Bud is crushed and determined to dethrone Kelly so he cleverly throws a wrench into the romance as well as Ashland's political career.

Peg playfully roughhousing with her exasperated husband..

The 14th episode of the fifth season is unusual in major ways. "Look Who's Barking" was told primarily from the viewpoint of Buck whose thoughts in this episode are voiced by Cheech Marin. Also, Katey Sagal never appears, but B. B. King, the legendary blues singer and musician, makes a cameo appearance.

The story starts with Buck feeling neglected by the Bundy family. He runs from the house to seek company. He finds a pretty female dog and leads her to the Bundy house. Buck bitterly regrets bringing the other canine home because Kelly and Bud shower the new dog with attention and ignore Buck.

Dog trainer Steve Ritt said that this episode required the most effort from Buck of any *MWC* episode. "Buck had to work with another dog, a little dog, in that episode," Ritt explains. "Buck was in every scene and you also had two dogs working together. In one scene, Buck had to work in time with King's music along with hitting several marks and performing tricks!"

Boom operator Scott I. Glickman has very fond memories of this particular episode: "I'll never forget one show that we did that Buck starred in that was a take-off on *Lady and the Tramp* and the premise was Buck running away and Buck hanging out with this female dog and the final scene you hear this bluesy guitar and you see B. B. King playing his guitar. That was an amazing night. After we filmed and the audience left,

B.B. King and the rest of the cast and crew went out together and we all had a great night."

The 20th Episode of Season 5 is worthy of note because it was the pilot for the short-lived spin-off series *Top of the Heap*. The episode bore the title "Top of the Heap" and had Al's old high school buddy, Charlie (Joseph Bologna), at a high society fundraiser with his dim-witted son Vinnie (Matt LeBlanc).

Perhaps the most significant aspect of Season 5 was Marcy's marriage to Jefferson D'Arcy. Her second married name was chosen as a play on the name of *The Cosby Show*'s Executive Director, Marcy Carsey. Season 5 was also the first time the fictional *Psycho Dad* was mentioned as Al's favorite TV program. This season also witnessed the first time his high school high point of having scored four touchdowns in one game was mentioned. The show's emphasis on Al's football glory days had parallels to Ed O'Neill's real life. He had attended Ohio University on a football scholarship. When he transferred to Youngstown State University after his sophomore year, he got a position on the school football team as a defensive lineman. In 1969, the Pittsburgh Steelers actually drafted O'Neill—although they cut him in training camp.

SEASON 6: THE SHOW GOES ON AND HOW!

The sixth season was strongly influenced by something going on with Katey Sagal in real life: she was pregnant by the time filming began. As a result, the writers decided on a storyline in which Peg got pregnant. The season opened with the two-part episode: "She's Having My Baby."

When Marcy and Jefferson visit the Bundy house, she is super-excited, hopping around like a bunny rabbit as she exclaims, "We're having a baby!" Al grins and gleefully teases Jefferson, telling him life is all over for him as he gets mired in the responsibilities of fatherhood. Then Peg crushes Al's enthusiasm with her announcement, "I'm pregnant too!"

Part 2 is more of the same. Al and Jefferson decide to make a run for it. They commiserate at a bar/bus station combo as they ogle semi-nude young women and talk about fleeing to freedom. Inevitably, however, both return to their pregnant wives.

Peg and Marcy are both depicted as pregnant through Episode 10. However, Peg does not appear (except in a photograph or painting) in Episodes 7-10. This is because Sagal was late into a pregnancy that had sadly become medically troubled. She suffered a stillbirth six weeks before her due date.

When Peg returns in "Al, The Shoe Dick," Al has a dream in which he acts as a private eye and solves the case of the "Pharaoh's Eye Diamond." In that dream, former porn actress turned mainstream actress Traci Lords makes an appearance. When Al awakens he is disappointed to learn it was only a dream. However, he is wonderfully relieved to discover that Peg's pregnancy was also just a dream! Marcy's pregnancy is also said to have just been a figment of Al's dream. Another significant part of this episode is that it Bud decided to try for a rap career as "Grandmaster B."

Bud's efforts as Grandmaster B paralleled Faustino's own attempts to start a hip-hop career. Faustino recalls, "Basically, everything that I would do in my outside life ended up in the script, whether it was my battle with zits, or just growing up."

One point that occasionally was underlined was that for all the conflict and disappointment in the Bundy marriage, love held it together. That point was made is Season 6's Episode 12.

In the oddly appropriate title "So This Is How Sinatra Felt," Al comes home in an unusually upbeat mood. He reveals that a pretty woman has been coming into the store and flirting with him and calls her "a shoe groupie." Peg is instantly aghast, fearful that Al is committing adultery. "Your father's cheating on me!" she wails to Bud and Kelly. Al declares his faithfulness. However, Peg assigns Bud and Kelly to sneak into the shoe store and spy on their Dad. They crouch behind the counter as he spends much time idle. Bud and Kelly consider leaving. Just then, a truly beautiful and sensuously attired woman (the famous Jessica Hahn) enters the store. She is carrying a tray of muffins. *The Shoe Groupie!* When Bud and Kelly get home, they report that there is a shoe groupie and she flirts with Al. However, as Kelly bluntly puts it, "They didn't have intercourse or anything." Al arrives home.

Toward the end of the episode, Al asserts to Peg, "I did not and never would cheat on you. I did have the opportunity though." Peg realizes that he really loves her and that they are meant for each other. The episode ends with Al depressed but he and Peg are holding each other.

Dick Warlock, a very experienced and busy stunt performer, worked on four episodes of *MWC*. The first was Season 6's Episode 16, "Rites of Passage."

It is Bud's 18th birthday. Peg plans a kid's birthday party for him, complete with clown. However, Bud is happier with Al's plan: a trip to the Nudie Bar. Thus, Bud celebrates his entrance into adulthood with a bar fight! Warlock recalled, "I played a bar patron who got into a piece of business with David Faustino. First, he beats me in the stomach and as

Glum Al pressured by Peg and Bud.

the girl walks by and gets his attention, he drops me face first on the floor. Later on in the fight, he and Ed [O'Neill] were back to back and as I moved toward him, he hit me over the head with a beer bottle that took me out."

During episode 17, entitled "The Egg and I," David Garrison made a return to the show as Steve Rhoades. "I always enjoyed revisiting the show, and discovering what Steve had been up to from year to year," he explained. Indeed, Garrison would make at least one appearance as Steve per year for a few years after he exited from the show. Each time Steve reappeared, he would be in a different line of work.

BEARING THE TITLE "The Goodbye Girl," Episode 22 was significant for what Kelly "achieved" during it. She gets a job at a theme park. Kelly is overflowing with enthusiasm when she informs Bud and Mom that she is a "paid employee of TV World Theme Park." Peg is disappointed that Kelly has a job since the Wanker family tradition is to leave work to men. However, Kelly soon discovers that jobs are not all glamour. Her job is to stand in a blue suit, endlessly waving and repeating, "Thank you, and come again." Marcy and Jefferson D'Arcy visit the theme park where children gather around Jefferson, asking him if he acted in *Happy Days* and in *The Love Boat*. Jefferson says "no." The in-joke of course was that actor Ted McGinley appeared on *Happy Days* as Roger Phillips and on *The Love Boat* as Ashley Covington Evans.

Luckily for Kelly, she is re-assigned to become the "Verminator," a kind of cartoon action heroine with a red cape who attacks people in cockroach costumes with a peculiar spray. Bud is hired as "King Roach" and performs in a bulky brown King Roach costume complete with multiple arms. The episode ends with Al cuddling Peg and the bizarrely costumed kids as he declares, "There's nothing like being home with a nice normal family."

The sixth season of *MWC* ended with a *three*-part episode that told what was indisputably one of the most outrageously creative stories of the entire series. It consisted of: "England Show: Part 1," "England Show: Part 2 Wastin' - The Company's Money," and "England Show: Part 3 - We're Spending As Fast As We Can." The 3-parter was a delightful excursion into horror/fantasy comedy.

Part 1 begins with a sign across the screen telling the audience that we are in "Lower Uncton England 1653." Ed O'Neill plays a blacksmith who insults a heavyset woman (Helena Carroll) despite her declaration that she is "a great and powerful witch." His continued ridicule of her weight leads the witch to exclaim, "I curse Seamus McBundy and all his male descendants! I curse Lower Uncton which will be in darkness as long as male Bundys live!"

A sign tells us we are back in 1992. However, Lower Uncton is apparently in a kind of time freeze, its residents garbed in the clothing characteristic of the time some four centuries prior when their town was cursed with darkness. We learn that the townspeople are determined to lift that curse. To that end, they have been luring male Bundys to the town and killing them. Now there are only two left: Al and Bud. The scene shifts to Peg who is understandably excited to receive a letter informing her that the Bundy family has won an all-expenses paid trip to England—with a stopover in a quant little town called Lower Uncton. The Bundy family travels to England. While Lower Uncton's townspeople plot to murder Al and Bud in their darkened town to lift its curse, big shots in the neighboring village of Upper Uncton plot to murder the pair in their town so that Lower Uncton will forever remain in darkness and Upper Uncton will continue to reap the benefits of being a tourist trap next to the darkened village.

Part 2 has the Bundys blissfully unaware of the plots against them as they enjoy their British vacation. The Bundys merrily shop in London even as an Upper Uncton assassin stalks them. While most of the family goes to Lower Uncton, Kelly stays behind in London because she is entranced with the city. However, someone warns Kelly that her family is in danger and that she must find her way to Lower Uncton to prevent the deaths of her Dad and brother. Needless to say, it hardly looks good for Al and Bud that pea-brained Kelly constitutes their only hope for survival!

In the concluding Part 3, Al challenges experienced horse rider Igor (Steven Hartley) to a joust. At first, Igor is clearly on his way to victory as Al is quite clumsy. However, Al takes a shoe off and holds the malodorous item before the nose of the horse upon which Igor rides. The horse throws the rider off and Al wins! Surprisingly, the Bundy victory lifts the curse and, for the first time in centuries, Lower Uncton is bathed in sunshine.

SEASON 7: NOT HEAVEN BUT TRULY SEVEN

DURING THE SEVENTH SEASON, Moye took a leave of absence to work on other things. In addition, some critics began turning against the show because it was becoming increasingly repetitive. Perhaps this is why a fresh character was introduced at the beginning of Season 7.

The first episode of Season 7 is entitled, appropriately enough, "Magnificent Seven." Peg's cousin and his wife visit the Bundys. When they depart, they leave behind their six-year-old son Seven (Shane Sweet). Peg is enchanted with Seven while Al, Kelly, and Bud are annoyed by him. Many comic complications flow from this difference, not only in this episode but also in other early episodes in the season. For example, the plot of "Every Bundy Has a Birthday" revolves around Peg wanting to celebrate Seven's birthday but not knowing its date. Thus, she decides to celebrate it on Al's birthday. In "Al on the Rocks," Peg has sunk the financially troubled family deeper in debt with Seven's doctor visits. Al takes a moonlighting job as a bartender in a topless joint. However, this is a topless joint catering to women in which the bartender struts his stuff! Al is happy to be treated as a sex object until Jefferson covers for him one day, leading Al to lose the job to the younger and more attractive man.

The lack of regular sexual intimacy in the Bundy marriage is the focus of Episode 5, "What I Did for Love." Peg buys a series of slinky outfits, hoping to entice Al into lovemaking. Finally, she accedes to his real wishes and cooks him a steak. The happy husband happily makes love to his wife. However, when he expects food the next night, Peg informs him that all that cooking was not worth it for the five minutes of sex she had. The ravenous Al desperately but futilely begs her to slave away at the stove and promises he can "bring it up to six minutes!"

In Episode 9, "Rock of Ages," poor Al finds that bill collectors have taken an entire paycheck from him. The distressed Al enters a shoe

Jonathan Wolff, who wrote the music for Season 7's "Rock of Ages" episode, became a regular episodic music writer for *MWC* when Season 8 began and stayed until the series ended. Photograph courtesy of Jonathan Wolff.

selling contest. Al wins! The prize is a trip to Hawaii. Seven is left with the D'Arcys and Al, Peg, Kelly, and Bud go to Chicago's O'Hare Airport. Al masquerades as an aging rock star named Axel Bundy so that he and his family can socialize with six famous rock musicians. The six were real-life rock stars: Richie Havens, Spencer Davis, John Sebastian, Robby Krieger, Mark Lindsay, and Peter Noone. This was also the first episode in which *MWC* hired music writer Jonathan Wolff to write a song. At the beginning of Season 8, he would be hired to regularly write episodic music for the show and would remain onboard for its last four seasons. Wolff remembers, "I was first hired to write only the song '*We Are The*

Old.'" As he often would, he composed the music well in advance of the shooting of the scene in which it would be played. "For on camera singing or dancing, I needed to create the music recordings far enough in advance so the other departments (actors, dancers, choreographer, director, camera crew) had time to prepare for the shoot."

"Rock of Ages" led to an important and very welcome advance for Wolff's entertainment career. "This was my first assignment for *MWC* and I was onstage every day to rehearse our awesome guest cast of rock legends," he fondly recalls. "I got great vibes from the producers, the cast, and the crew. This was supposed to be just a one-time songwriting assignment, just for the episode. But I really wanted to be hired permanently onto the series. And when the next season started, *MWC* invited me to be a permanent member of the team."

One of the most memorable episodes of *MWC* is Season 7's Episode 18, "Peggy and the Pirates." In this episode, Peggy spins a bedtime story for Seven of lovely Princess Scarlett (Peg) and pirates on the high seas. We see it as Peg's fantasy; Al is her captor, Captain Courage, and Jefferson is her rescuer, Prince Paco. Marcy plays a cabin girl (who is mistaken for a cabin boy), Kelly is a slow-witted navigator, Bud is a hunchbacked first mate named Fluvio, and Steve Rhoades plays the odd part of Rubio the Cruel, whose cruelty consists primarily of his singing renditions of show tunes that are horrible on the ear.

When interviewed by this writer, David Garrison recalled this episode as his "favorite return" to the series because, "Playing Rubio the Cruel gave the writers (and me) ample opportunity to poke fun at my other life as a Broadway song and dance man." There was quite a bit of action in this episode. As stunt performer Dick Warlock noted, "I played a swashbuckler, who in the sword fight gets stuck in the breadbasket (stomach) and falls overboard."

In an interview with boom operator Scott I. Glickman, he revealed that he found the scene of the pirate ship "especially technically challenging." Why? "The ship's platform was up pretty high and there were a lot of actors talking all over the ship," he explained. "We had to pinpoint every actor for the booms, so it took more time to film than a usual show. Sometimes it was hard for the booms to reach the actor on the pirate ship, so instead of booms we used a few radio mikes to get the dialogue of an actor, like they often do in movies. We also used what is called a "fishpole," which is a handheld pole with a mike on the end of it, to get someone who was way up on the platform of the pirate ship."

Before Season 7 was over, it became apparent that *MWC* viewers were not warming to the character of Seven. He was pretty much written out of *MWC* without explanation, although in Season 8 a single, subtle reference to Seven would be made when his photograph is displayed as a missing child on a milk carton.

"Mr. Empty Pants" is the title of Episode 16 and the title captures the pitiful, albeit rollickingly funny, spirit of the story. Peg wants to take up a hobby and she draws a caricature of Al, which she names "Mr. Empty Pants." The cartoon becomes incredibly popular. Al is dismayed until he gets an offer from *Playgirl* magazine that would like to feature a photo of him. Then it is Peg's turn to be dismayed—no matter how much she derides her Al, he is *hers*.

The sue-happy nature of contemporary America is wickedly skewered in "Un-Alful Entry." A squabble with Peg leads Al to sleep on the couch. This happens to be the night that a burglar breaks into the Bundy home! While Al is asleep, that burglar (Randall "Tex" Cobb) brushes his butt against Al. The drowsy Al believes Peg is hinting for him to rub her bottom so he fondles the bottom of the burglar. Eventually, the burglar awakens Al, who runs the burglar out of the residence. Al is temporarily the neighborhood hero, until the burglar sues for distress! A court scene follows with the burglar demanding compensation from the people he burgled.

This season wound up with "The Proposition." An old girlfriend of Al's (Vanna White) has joined the ranks of the super-wealthy. But there is one thing she wants, Al. Can she buy him from Peg for $500,000? The episode ends on a touching note: Peg realizes that she loves that lug and will not part with him even for half a million dollars! Peg and Al belong together. Dysfunctional as the Bundy family is, love holds it together.

All in all, the appearance and disappearance of Seven was one of the most significant developments of this season. Another was Bud's oh-so-welcome loss of his virginity and his first appearance sporting beard growth. Finally, Al's chances to cheat but continued fidelity powerfully underscores the sense of loyalty that holds this often-squabbling couple together.

SEASON 8: BUNDY LIFE CONTINUES NOT-SO-GREAT

MOYE WAS BACK by Season 8. However, it would be the next-to-last season in which he and Leavitt would both work on the program.

MWC won a reputation for raunchiness and irreverence, but there was always a greater dimension to the groundbreaking sitcom. At the core of the program's impetus was the way it dealt with the disappointments intrinsic to human life.

Season 8's Episode 2 is entitled "Hood 'n The Boyz" and is a prime example of the way *MWC* spoke to so many people with its overall theme of youth's hopes unrealized. "Hood 'n The Boyz" manages to get all the laughs it wants, but at the same time function as a kind of meditation on the problems inherent in aging. There are reasons "*young* punk" rather than "middle-aged punk" is the usual expression. Late adolescence and early adulthood are periods of restlessness coupled with (at least for males) physical strength.

Al hears from a childhood sweetheart that a young punk has been bothering her at the convenience store at which she is currently employed. Will Al come to her rescue? At the store, Al's childhood friend, Mary Ellen Litchfield (Debra Engle), says she is asking for Al's help because the punk reminds her of Al when he was young. Just then the punk, Ray-Ray (Matt Borlenghi), saunters in—with a hand stuck down the front of his pants! He demands free food be served to him. Concerned for Mary Ellen and wanting to impress her as well as wanting to help her, Al soon challenges Ray-Ray to a fight. Ray-Ray, together with the young punks who hang around him, beat Al up. A battered Al recalls his high school days as "King of the Streets." He vows to round up his old gang so they can confront Ray-Ray and his band. But Al's old gang is now *old*. Paunchy and softened by time, they are no match for much younger men. Al's pals desert him and he is again beaten. However, a badly bruised Al comes back yet again to face Ray-Ray and his crew. Al explains that, as a man, he desperately wants to impress and aid a woman. When Ray-Ray and his fellow young punks realize that the next step is to murder Al, the youths cannot take that final step and walk away from Al, who basks in the gratitude of Mary Ellen. Al is disappointed when she tells him that, even had Al not been married, her gratitude would not have been accompanied by sexual favors. It is gratitude nonetheless and Al, brutalized and in pain, finds a wisp of satisfaction in it.

One of the most outrageous episodes in sitcom history must be Episode 5 in Season 8, "Banking on Marcy." It featured not just one, but two almost unbelievably hilarious scenes. We learn at the start that Marcy fears public speaking. Peg advises her to call "Dr. Angela" for advice. Marcy reports that the good doctor advised "transference," that is, for Marcy to try to put herself in a position in which she has no problem speaking. It just so happens that Marcy has no problem speaking when she is having sex. Thus, Marcy gives a public speech to bankers—and has a public orgasm!

To her surprise, this does not get her fired, but rather wins her a raise and assignments to keep giving speeches. The episode's second most hilarious scene is when Jefferson complains about their sex life suffering as a result of her work activities. Ignoring Al, Marcy and Jefferson sit with Al between them and describe in graphic detail what Jefferson calls their "rodeo nights." Al's face looks increasingly and dramatically sick. In this scene, Ed O'Neill more than earned his comic stripes—and without making a sound.

A noteworthy episode of Season 8 is Episode 9, "NO MA'AM," in which both feminism and traditionalism come in for a beautifully even-handed comic drubbing. The title is that of an organization Al forms.

This episode introduced new characters who would have recurring roles in the series. One of them was Bob Rooney, played by E. E. Bell. "The audition was most memorable," he told this author. "When they were going to launch the 'NO MA'AM' storyline, the casting call went out for character actors. The day I went in there were maybe 50 actors in the hall. They broke us up in groups of five. I guess they had a good eye because the group I was in all were on set when we shot the first 'NO MA'AM' story."

In this episode, Al is outraged that "The Masculine Feminist," Jerry Springer, helped a women's group create a ladies' night at the bowling alley he frequents on the night he likes to be there.

Al gets a bunch of guys together in his garage but they soon tire of bowling in the cramped space. One of the guys was Bob Rooney, played by E. E. Bell, who would become a regular in the series. They plan to go to the one place where "men can still be men": The Nudie Bar. However, they find out The Nudie Bar has been turned into a coffeehouse featuring a plump middle-aged woman reading her poetry! Al and the guys form a club they call "NO MA'AM" for *National Organization of Men Against Amazonian Masterhood*. The group dons Lone Ranger-style masks and takes over the program of "The Masculine Feminist." They tie Springer to a chair and threaten to perform what they call a sexorcism on him, in which they force him to watch wrestling. Marcy interrupts the show and calls the cops to back her up. Al ends up doing "community service" in The Nudie Bar-turned-coffee shop. However, Al gets the last laugh when someone pelts the poet, who is reciting poetry about her 'eggs,' with a raw egg.

Interviewed by this author, E. E. Bell recalled, "When you are a guest actor in a series, especially one that had been established so long before I got there, the challenge is to fit into the organization that has been established." However, Bell elaborates, "I must say the cast and crew were the most welcoming bunch it has been my pleasure to encounter. This made the challenge very easy to handle."

A wry comment on a common human frailty, that of overlooking those to whom we are close, is made in Episode 11, "Change for A Buck." This episode does not center on a dollar bill, but instead on the Bundy canine. Once again, Buck the dog feels badly neglected. The unhappy canine runs away from home, but is soon sorry because he finds himself caged in a shelter. He becomes even more sorry when he learns that dogs are killed after seven days in that shelter. Meanwhile, the Bundys do not even notice that their dog is gone for a total of six days. Finally, Peg asks Al and Bud if they have "noticed anything missing." Kelly says she went walking with Buck's leash and realized she was "Buck naked." The Bundy family rescues Buck right before he would have been put to death.

A comment on the nature of the Bundy marriage and the feelings Al and Peg have for each other is made in "Honey, I Blew Myself Up," Episode 15 of Season 8. As a birthday present for Al, Peg has a photographer take a sexy picture of her. The photographer blows the photo up and posts a billboard size version of it across from the shoe store where Al works. Al is unwilling to admit to Peg that having men admire her photo makes him jealous, so he enlists the help of a group of rabid women's lib extremists, led by his nemesis, Marcy, to protest the alleged exploitation of a woman's body.

The next episode, Episode 16, is "How Green Was My Apple?" and might be regarded as of special interest because it recalls other sitcoms through its guest actors. A dispute over whether an apple from a tree in the Bundy yard which had its limb hanging into the D'Arcy yard actually belonged to the Bundys or the D'Arcys escalates into an all-out war over the property line. Dave Madden, who became famous as the manager on the wholesome 1970s sitcom *The Partridge Family*, Danny Bonaduce, known as the endearingly mischievous Danny Partridge on that same sitcom, and Gary Coleman, once the lovable little Arnold on the late 70s-early 80s sitcom *Diff'rent Strokes*. play small parts in this episode. Bonaduce and Coleman are recognized, but deny they are who they are. As it previously did by having Jerry Mathers, who shot to fame as the Beaver on that widely beloved classic sitcoms, *Leave It To Beaver*, appear on it, *MWC* sardonically commented on previous sitcoms by featuring adults who had made their names as child actors in traditionally "clean" sitcoms.

As it had with "Married... with Aliens," *MWC* once again forayed into science fiction comedy in Episode 19, "Field of Screams." Kelly, as The Verminator, sprays Buck and Bud with a new poison called Springtime in Baghdad. Buck morphs into a different breed of dog and then into a turkey; Bud grows breasts. The second storyline, and the one that gives the episode its title, is that Marcy and her bank have sold Polk High's football field to a foreign company so they can build a factory there. Al objects to this as a violation of his heritage and chains himself to a goalpost as a protest. Although his protest leads the company to move its factory, the loss to the community is such that Al's victory leaves his family and friends hanging their heads in shame.

Episode 23 is "The Legend of Ironhead Haynes." Just as *MWC* ribbed both feminists and anti-feminists, it also took pokes at both modern-day political correctness and attempts to counter it. This episode was one of *MWC*'s most hilarious takes on both political correctness and its enemies. Fed up with contemporary hyper-sensitivity, Al and the NO MA'AM group decide to seek the guidance of a man who has become a kind of legend, Ironhead Haynes.

Supposedly the roughest and toughest male to ever graduate from Polk High, Ironhead Haynes is said to live in solitude atop a mountain. Al and the other NO MA'AM members head for the hills. However, as they approach the mountain, Roger (Chris Latta) has second thoughts, suggesting that the legend of Ironhead Haynes might be just that, a legend with no basis in truth. The men are obviously scared to continue up the mountain. Only Al has the gumption—or just plain foolishness—to continue. He reaches Ironhead Haynes, who is played by country and western music legend Waylon Jennings. Al explains how he and other men need Ironhead's wisdom because of the strains caused by political correctness: "Old people get mad if you call them old, foreign people get mad if you tell them to go home, and the slightest thing will set a gimp off." Ironhead concludes that Al wants to know what can be done about it. He takes a guitar into his hands and sings one word: "Nothing!"

What does the family want from Dad?

Perhaps what is most notable about Season 8 was that some of Al's buddies were either introduced during the season or first prominent during it. Characters like NO MA'AMers Bob Rooney and Roger, as well as coworker Aaron (Hill Harper) would be seen fairly frequently in future episodes, as would Officer Dan. Although Officer Dan was introduced as a character in Season 8, the actor who played him, Dan Tullis Jr., had previously appeared on *MWC*—always as a law enforcement professional: a cop issuing Al a ticket in "Rock 'n Roll Girl" for having an insulting bumper sticker; a cop arresting Al in "Weenie Tot Lovers and Other Strangers"; an FBI agent searching for Steve Rhoades in "The Egg and I."

In an interview with this author, Tullis speculates as to why *MWC* always cast him as a law enforcement officer. "It appears that I have a rather commanding, authoritative voice—as did my father, the Air Force Sergeant and Baptist pastor—and a kind of no nonsense demeanor, when I need it," he observes. After playing those first couple of roles, they told me the Bundys would be in trouble a lot so they wanted to have them interact with the 'law' often." Thus, *MWC* cast Tullis as a Chicago police officer.

In addition, Season 8 has Bud being accepted into a college fraternity. As previously observed, there is an odd suggestion through having Seven's photo on a milk carton that he disappeared from the series because he was kidnapped.

Late in the eighth season and early in the ninth, Katey Sagal was again pregnant in real life. The scriptwriters did not write this pregnancy into the storyline, but filmed her in such a way as to hide her swelling belly from the audience. Luckily, this pregnancy did not end sadly, but instead in the birth of her baby.

This was also the season in which, right from the start, Jonathan Wolff was hired to write episodic music on a regular basis for the show, a position he would keep until the show went off the air. He very much enjoyed his work on the program. In an interview with this author, Wolff recalls, "My years as the episodic music composer on *Married... with Children* included some of the funniest, wackiest assignments of my entire career. I have only warm fuzzies from that show and the awesome team of people who worked so well together to make it." Discussing what being an episodic composer requires, he explains, "About a week before an episode begins shooting, each production department receives a script so they can prepare (wardrobe, props, set dressing…). I would read the script and database my 'to-do' list of music pieces and/or on-stage music assistance that this episode might need."

SEASON 9: MOYE AND LEAVITT ALL DOWN THE LINE

THE VENUE AT WHICH *MWC* was taped changed from Hollywood to Culver City, California for Season 9, and would remain there for the duration of the show. *Budyology* reports, "The Bundy living room was a permanent set on stage 28 at Sony Pictures Studios."

One of the more interesting early episodes of the ninth season was Episode 4, "Naughty but Niece." Marcy's pretty niece, Amber (Juliet Tablak), visits the D'Arcys. Bud gets a major-league crush on her, which pays off for him when he actually gets to have sex with Amber. Bud has a fantasy scene that is shot in black and white of him in a ballroom with Amber. Wolff told this writer this was a scene for which he crafted the music in advance so the other departments could prepare for the shoot with it in mind.

The most remarkable of the early episodes in the ninth season of *MWC* was, at least in this writer's opinion, a two-part episode: Episode 5, "Business Sucks," and Episode 6, "Business Still Sucks." Of course, there is a double meaning to sucks, but in this case the second meaning does not refer to oral sex; it refers to breast-feeding. A mom comes into the store holding a baby and breastfeeds the baby; Al and Griff are repulsed. Griff commands her to "ooze on down the road." Marcy and her women's group stage a breastfeed-a-thon at the store. This leads to a counter-demonstration by Al and the NO MA'AM group, who retaliate by taking off their shirts and shaking their beer bellies. It is quite a sight!

This episode introduced a *MWC* character who would appear again more than once on the program—reporter Miranda Veracruz de la Hoya Cardinal (Teresa Parente), who was at the shoe store to cover the breastfeed-a-thon for a news program. Perhaps Parente's greatest accomplishment as the often-exasperated reporter was to rapidly state her name, making a kind of joke out of her very multi-syllabic moniker.

Al tried to dispense fatherly wisdom but was never Lincolnesque.

Part 2 includes Al discovering that the owner of the shoe store, Gary, is a woman (played by Janet Carroll). Bud tells Al that the courts have ruled women have a legal right to breastfeed in public. Al looks with resigned disgust on the women breastfeeding but says he will draw the line at diaper changes. The episode ends with a bunch of women dangling dirty diapers in front of a comically defeated Al.

The episode following this one is "Dial B for Virgin." It is typical of a kind of "virgin-phobia" in *MWC*. Bud wants extra credit in college so he signs up for community service. He was hoping for a "save the rainforest" campaign that would allow him to ogle Brazilian women. The only thing open was a hotline for virgins suffering temptation. The episode milks the conflict between Bud's horniness and the nature of the service for all its worth, along with the odd humiliation he suffers for being part of a service that champions abstinence.

Episode 9 is "No Pot to Pease In." It is magnificently and courageously meta-referential. Kelly goes to audition for a new FOX sitcom entitled *Pease in a Pod*. During the audition, she talks about her own family with the TV executives. She does not get a part in the show, but when her family sees the premiere they realize that the Peases have been modeled after the Bundys. The Bundys go to the studio to complain about the stealing of Kelly's recollections. A TV honcho hands Al $500 and promises him that amount for every episode. However, the show is canceled after the pilot. Marcy explains, "Some woman in Michigan didn't like it"—an unmistakable poke at Terry Rakolta. *The Family Keats*, apparently a saccharine show about a goody-goody 18th century family, replaces *Pease in a Pod*. In an interview with this writer, Wolff disclosed that he wrote theme songs for both *Pease in a Pod* and *The Family Keats*, and describes that of *The Family Keats* as "silly Baroque opera." He also told this writer,

"Veteran studio singer Angie Jaree performed both *Pease in a Pod* and *Family Keats* theme songs for that episode."

Among the most endearingly outrageous episodes of Season 9 are the two-part episode, "I Want My *Psycho Dad*." In Episode 12, Al learns that his favorite TV show, *Psycho Dad*, has been canceled. Who is responsible? Al declares, "Marcy D'Arcy, Chicken At Large." Marcy's group, FANG (Feminists Against Neanderthal Guys), had agitated against *Psycho Dad* and succeeded in getting the program canceled. Al vows that he and the NO MA'AM bunch will go to Washington D.C. to testify before Congress about why the show should be brought back.

Episode 13 is "I Want My Psycho Dad: Second Blood." The NO MA'AMers get to Washington D.C., and men (who, it is suggested, are buddies from Jefferson's supposed CIA derring-do days) gag and tie up Marcy and Peg to allow the NO MA'AM crew to testify before the Senate. The NO MA'AM members appropriately make fools of themselves, but the episode ends without a revival of the canceled *Psycho Dad*; Al loses again.

Sometimes *MWC* could be so outrageous it made it difficult for crew members to do their jobs. Such was Season 9's Episode 14, "The Naked and the Dead, But Mostly the Naked." Peggy and other neighborhood wives want to see what their husbands do at The Jiggly Room. Al agrees that the wives may accompany the men to the place, but on Thursday night because it is A-cup night at the strip bar. Things go all right for the fellows until a special act comes out, that of a super-voluptuous stripper called Rocki Mountains, and played by the extraordinarily big-breasted Letha Weapons.

Talking to this author, boom operator Scott I. Glickman laughingly recalls that she "had the biggest breasts I'd ever seen in my life." He continues, "In the scene in which she is dancing on stage and Al is in the audience with Peggy and Marcy and Jefferson, I clicked on the headset and said that if she takes off that top I can't guarantee that I can boom that scene! She took the top off and she threw it on Al and the cup basically covered his whole head. When she took the bra off, I missed a line with the boom because my jaw was on the ground! I was so shocked by the size of her breasts and her nipples."

The wives end up benefiting from the strip club entertainment. We see the outside of homes and hear a succession of clearly satisfied female voices moaning: "Oh, Charlie!" "Oh, Ike!" "Oh, Bob Rooney!" "Oh, Al!" "Oh, Mr. Lincoln!"

A word should be said about the aforementioned (afore-moaned?) names. The last, Mr. Lincoln, is moaned by Marcy in reference to Jefferson, who put an Abe Lincoln-style beard on himself for The Jiggly Room visit. He hoped the beard would mean that the workers there would fail to recognize him so Marcy would not know he was a regular visitor to the joint. Of course, someone does recognize him and he tries to pooh-pooh it to Marcy.

Perhaps the most startling moan is "Oh, Bob Rooney!" One quirk associated with the program's treatment of the Bob Rooney character is that he was *always* referred to by both first and last name. This writer asked E. E. Bell, the actor who played Bob Rooney, why this character is inevitably referred to this way. "I asked Michael Moye this very same question," Bell recalls. "He said that when growing up, in every neighborhood he lived in, there was always one guy you always called by both names. To have his wife do it too was just plain funny."

Bell noted that working on scenes filmed in The Jiggly Room were a special perk of being an actor on the program. "All the scenes in The Jiggly Room were very enjoyable to film," he explains. "Surrounded by beautiful half-naked women and getting paid for it. I mean, come on!"

"Get the Dodge Outta Hell," Episode 16, was one of the more significant episodes of Season 9. The Bundys go to a car wash to clean the Dodge, and are told that the Dodge has somehow been lost! The carwash offers to give Al a new car. The family is OK with that but Al says nothing doing. He must have the old car because it has something in its trunk that he must have. "*Big 'Uns*," Peg speculates. As it turns out, the Dodge is still there. It is just that people could not recognize it after it was cleaned and the color appeared to change from orange to red. Al opens the trunk of the car to ensure that the item he treasures is there. He takes out an issue of *Big 'Uns*. Then he opens the magazine to remove from its pages a large photograph of the Bundy family. "Awww," the audience knowingly sighs. Al Bundy really does love, cherish, and even take pride in his family.

E. E. Bell told this author that his favorite *MWC* episode is Episode 22 of Season 9, "User Friendly." In this episode, Al finds an electrical switch but does not know what the function of it is. His obsession with finding out its function leads him, together with Jefferson, to wreak havoc on his house's electrical wiring. Bob Rooney comes over to save the day. Peg sardonically comments, "Bob Rooney is a butcher." Al points out that Bob Rooney owns a set of books dedicated to electrical wiring. When Bob Rooney admits that, at the behest of his wife he sent the books back,

Al says, "But not before you read them on the john!" Bob Rooney then exclaims, "Do you know me or what?" What ends up happening? Bob Rooney gets stuck in the walls of the Bundy house! Bell remarks, "Judging from reactions I get, it seems to be a favorite episode with many fans."

April 30, 1995 saw the broadcast of "Special: My Favorite *Married*." In this special episode, Ed O'Neill, Katey Sagal, Christina Applegate, David Faustino, David Garrison, and Ted McGinley discuss their favorite *MWC* scenes.

The next episode broadcast was unusual on two counts—it featured Garrison and it was a pilot for a spin-off. Entitled "Radio Free Trumaine," set in the college Bud attends, the fictional Trumaine University, and it has disc jockeys Oliver Cole (Eric Dane) and Mark Campbell (Andrew Kavovit) interviewing the school's new dean of students, who is none other than Steve Rhoades. The dean is outraged when the youths disclose that he had been a chauffer only two months before settling into his present job. Rhoades causes both Oliver and Mark to not only lose their radio jobs but to be expelled from Trumaine. When Marcy hears about what her ex-husband did to the students, she leads a protest against it.

The series for which "Radio Free Trumaine" was the proposed pilot would have been about the student radio station at Trumaine University. However, the pilot failed to lead to an actual series.

Among the highlights of Season 9 were two appearances by David Garrison reprising his role as Steve Rhoades, the introduction of Al's shoe store co-worker, Griff, who was played by Harold Sylvester, and Bud's getting a driving examiner job. Already mentioned highlights were the first appearance of shoe store owner Gary, the cancellation of Al's beloved *Psycho Dad*, and the first appearances of Marcy's niece, Amber, and fast-talking TV reporter Miranda Veracruz de la Hoya Cardinal.

Behind the scenes, cast and crew continued to work cooperatively to put on the show and to occasionally have fun together afterwards. Looking back on his time working for *MWC*, Jonathan Wolff told this writer that what he liked most was the people. Wolff noted, "The *MWC* crew was a well-tuned Delta Force of elite experienced production professionals… who were also nice folks."

E. E. Bell says, "The funniest part of the week was the first reading of the script, all of us just sitting around the table having a great time." When Season 9 ended, Leavitt left the program for good.

SEASON 10: IN-LAWS AND OTHER OUTRAGES

THE TENTH SEASON OF *MWC* got off to an uproarious start with "Guess Who's Coming to Breakfast, Lunch and Dinner." The audience was introduced to both Peg's mom (Kathleen Freeman) and her dad, Ephraim Wanker (Tim Conway). Peg's mom and dad have had a falling out, so Mom has arrived at the Bundy house. As would be true whenever Peg's mom is around, she is *never* seen, and only heard. This is because much of the humor revolves about her being extraordinarily, it is suggested almost inhumanly, fat. Showing a fat woman would inevitably be disappointing, as she could never be as humongous as the program suggested, so the audience is left to continually imagine this gargantuan creature. Freeman was the perfect choice for the role as her gravelly, rather deep voice easily sounded comically ominous.

Garbed in classic hillbilly clothing, Conway is equally perfect as the good-hearted rube to whom the enormous woman is married. Peg is distraught at being from a "broken home" and insists Al go to Wanker County to persuade Ephraim to reclaim his wife. Al finds Ephraim, brings him to the Bundy house, and the Wankers reconcile by the end of the episode.

Buck had acted in *MWC* since the pilot and was getting up in dog years by Season 10. The decision to retire the canine actor led to the storyline of that season's Episode 3. This episode of exuberantly otherworldly humor is divided into parallel plotlines. Buck has died, and his death has hit Kelly especially hard. Much of the episode is devoted to the efforts to comfort the often-crying Kelly. The other part of the episode features Buck finding himself in a comical afterlife. He is among clouds when informed that he is "where animals go when they die." The "voice" of Buck exclaims, "I'm in Oprah's refrigerator!" He learns he is in a supernatural waiting room. If Buck has been a "good" dog, he may go to heaven. If not… Episodic composer Jonathan Wolff told this writer that this was an example of a time "when I added music as a comedic device on *MWC*." He wrote what he calls a "Doggie Heaven underscore" for this scene. Things do not look good for Buck when he finds out the judge who will decide his fate is a cat!

The Bundys and D'Arcys hope to help Kelly cheer up by having a séance, at which the spirit of Buck is summoned. The séance is led by Father Guido Sarducci, a character created and played by Don Novello on *Saturday Night Live*. It turns out that Judge Felix the Cat has sentenced Buck to be reincarnated as the second dog of the Bundy family. Thus, a cocker spaniel puppy materializes in the Bundy household. The little dog is named Lucky.

The episode ends with a sign appearing in which it is proclaimed this episode is "Dedicated to Buck the Dog, who will be enjoying a well-deserved retirement." In real life, Buck died about eight months after "Requiem" was aired, on May 28, 1998. He was thirteen years old, elderly for a dog.

Talking to this writer, Steven Ritt makes it clear that training Lucky presented different challenges from training Buck. "Lucky was a puppy when he started," Ritt explains. "Training techniques for a puppy are different because their attention spans are shorter. You have to work more with kid gloves when you work with a puppy." However, Ritt adds that Lucky was an alert and competent dog actor. "He did everything really well, even as a puppy," Ritt comments. "He was hitting two marks along with performing multiple tricks on silent cues in the same scene with no cuts."

MWC took being irreverent to a new high, or low, depending on one's viewpoint, in Episode 4, "Reverend Al." This episode brilliantly skewers religious hypocrisy. To avoid paying income tax, NO MA'AM becomes a church. "Reverend Al" appears in front of his congregation in flowing multi-colored robes and with his hair in a stiff pompadour. He is flanked by two scantily-clad "altar vixens." However, he is unmasked by Marcy, who displays photographs showing that Al has—gasp!—romanced Peg, the woman to whom he is married. Close to tears, Reverend Al confesses, "I have sinned. I have consorted with my wife. Let he who is without wife cast the first stone." A rock is hurled and Al is knocked out. Shades of the sex scandals surrounding such famous televangelists as Jim Bakker and Jimmy Swaggert hover humorously over this episode.

Season 10, Episode 7 has the title "Flight of the Bumblebee." This is the second and last *MWC* episode in which King Kong Bundy acted. In

I'm thinking, I'm thinking…

this episode he plays himself, the wrestler King Kong Bundy. The episode is about Bud's attempt to get into NO MA'AM. Al informs Bud that the Bundy family is not related to the wrestler. He also tells Bud that he can get into NO MA'AM if he gets his picture taken beside King Kong Bundy. Bud dresses as a Bumblebee in a bid to get the famous wrestler to stand beside him, and ends up getting mistaken for another wrestler! Poor little Bud ends up in the ring "fighting" the aptly named King Kong Bundy.

"Love Conquers Al" is Episode 12. Al agrees to take part in a New Age-type marriage counseling group in hopes that the counseling will lead his father-in-law and mother-in-law to reconcile, thus getting the latter out of his house. In a curious role reversal, Bud finds himself with a sexually available woman while Kelly is stuck with a handsome man who wants to get to know her rather than have sex. Kelly's frustration is played for laughs, but it is not so much humorous as perversely sad. It also seems like another instance in which *MWC* displayed a kind of abstinence phobia.

Episode 13, "I Can't Believe It's Butter," is a hilarious send-up of the phone sex industry. Al's buddies call a sensuous phone sex operator named Butter. Then Al discovers that the sexy-sounding Butter is none other than his enormously fat and usually gruff-sounding mother-in-law! This becomes even more hilarious when Griff confides that he believes he has fallen in love with Butter.

Perhaps the most significant development in Season 10 was the "death" of Buck and his replacement by Lucky. The first appearances of Peg's in-laws were also very significant with the caveat that Peg's mother-in-law never visually "appears" so the audience can only imagine her comically gargantuan dimensions.

Season 10 also saw another real-life Katey Sagal pregnancy. Once again, the writers did not put in a Peg pregnancy, and Sagal's pregnancy was hidden from the television audience by having the cameras avoid her belly. In real life, this pregnancy ended happily with a birth.

Most of those working on the show continued to get along famously backstage and offstage. In an interview with this writer, E. E. Bell could recall no instance of anything upsetting when he worked on *MWC*. "It was such a well-run organization that it all unfolded very smoothly," Bell declares. According to Dan Tullis, Jr., "It was the best set (tied by *Rachel Gunn, RN*, another series I did during the '91-'92 seasons) I had the privilege to 'work' on. Friction was minimal and the cast were like hosts at a nice dinner party. They welcomed guests and treated performers as virtual equals and celebs as the icons they often were. All concerned worked to produce the highest quality effort they could, and it paid off."

SEASON 11: LAST BUT NOT LEAST...

THE ELEVENTH *MWC* SEASON would turn out to be its last. The show was still funny but the tropes and jokes were becoming repetitive and, by Season 11, the ratings were going down. Indeed, even before the last season the show often seemed to descend into a kind of self-parody.

One very much repeated trope of the show was underlined in "Kelly's Gotta Habit," Episode 3 of the final season: the program's previously mentioned abstinence/virgin phobia. As Kelly's agent, Bud secured a role for her in a television commercial as a nun. Garbed in a nun's habit, she holds what she calls "Extra, extra virgin olive oil," and adds, "It's pure—like me!" Obviously, there is a hilarious irony here as sexiness is a Kelly Bundy trademark. The olive oil is manufactured by a group of Roman Catholic nuns and the contract for the actress who represents them in the television commercial requires she abstain from sex for as long as she works on the campaign. Needless to say, Kelly finds this difficult, very difficult, and many laughs are wrung from her sexual frustration.

Episodes 4 and 5 were a two-parter entitled "Requiem for a Chevyweight." Gary Grubbs, the actor who played Delbert in Season 2's "Poppy's by the Tree," appeared in the second part of "Chevyweight." Grubbs told this author, "In most shows, you do one episode and you don't do another one, but that show thought we're all actors, we're all pretending, so they broke that rule like they broke other rules. I didn't audition for it but was just hired to play a used car salesman who tries to trick Al into buying a used car."

The sexual boredom of the Bundy marriage, and Al's wish to avoid what has become a dull duty, is underlined in Episode 7, "The Juggs Have Left the Building." Peg wants to vacation in Branson, Missouri. Al pooh-poohs the idea until Peg informs him that the hotel in which they might stay only has rooms with twin beds. "Peg, saddle up and lasso the young 'uns, we're Branson bound!" Al declares. The show has a parallel plot in which *MWC* brilliantly makes fun of itself. Marcy and Jefferson decide to do sexual role-playing—as Peg and Al! The sight of Marcy in a Peg red bouffant wig and Jefferson in an Al bland blue shirt and brown slacks is hysterically humorous.

MWC also makes fun of itself in Episode 10, "The Stepford Peg," a take-off on both *The Stepford Wives* and Peg's leisurely style of being a housewife. Peg hits her head, the trauma giving her amnesia. Al then convinces her that she has been an industrious, June Cleaver-style housewife. Peg gets her memory back when they start having sex and she is outraged that Al has been getting her to do so much housework.

On February 24, 1997, two parts of a special three-part *MWC* episode were broadcast. The title was "Breaking Up Is Easy to Do." At the suggestion of the D'Arcys, Al and Peg see a marriage counselor. After seeing the counselor who was supposed to help mend their marriage, Al and Peg break up! Al moves out of the house and Peg begins dating another man. In Part 3, Al tries to date other women but has poor luck. At the end of the third part, Al and Peg reconcile. They realize that regardless of their problems, they belong together.

Episode 20, "Damn Bundys," is a delightfully outrageous *MWC* exploration in horror-comedy. Al makes a pact with none other than the devil. In exchange for Al's soul, Lucifer has Al play with the Chicago Bears and take them to the Super Bowl! Significantly, actor Robert Englund, who won fame for depicting film super-monster Freddy Krueger in the *Nightmare on Elm Street* film series, plays the devil in this *MWC* episode. Of course, Al does not want to quit after his goal has been achieved, but the devil sends him to Hades with the rest of his family. Al's afterlife in Hell turns out to be, in his opinion, amazingly similar to his life on Earth! Al challenges the devil to a football match to allow Al and his family to return to life on earth.

The next episode plays with the reality of the life of Amanda Bearse. Bearse is a lesbian and the title of Episode 21 is "Lez Be Friends." Wearing a black wig, Bearse plays the part of Marcy's lesbian cousin, Mandy, who comes to visit Marcy. However, Marcy is unaware of Mandy's sexual preferences so she asks Al to help keep Mandy away from Jefferson.

The two-part episode that starts with Episode 22, entitled "The Desperate Half-Hour" and winds up with Episode 23, "How To Marry A Moron," is often regarded as the "true" or "real" *MWC* last episode—even though Episode 23 was not the last episode broadcast.

In Episode 22, we learn that Bud has been corresponding with a young woman prison inmate named Starla (Tricia Cast). He looks forward to seeing her, believing she has just been paroled. She comes into the Bundy house, and is soon waving a gun. She has not been released but has escaped and holds the Bundy family plus the D'Arcys hostage in the Bundy home. After a brief period, Starla's boyfriend, Lonnie (Charles Esten), comes into the house as well. Lonnie is mentally dense enough to believe she was paroled through a drainpipe! Lonnie loses interest in Starla and finds himself powerfully attracted to Kelly, who is also strongly attracted to him. At the end of the episode, Starla and Lonnie are arrested and taken away. However, as Lonnie is being taken away, he proposes marriage to Kelly and she accepts that proposal.

Lonnie has been (legitimately) released at the start of Episode 23, "How to Marry A Moron," And he wants to wed Kelly. Al tries to strangle the ex-convict and bangs Lonnie's head against the wall. Lonnie then mentions that his last name is "Tot"; he is a member of the wealthy family that manufactures Weenie Tots—one of Al's favorite foods! Al is overjoyed at the prospect of having a man from such a family as a son-in-law! The wedding does not come off because, on the very day of the wedding, Lonnie makes advances to, of all people, Marcy.

The last *MWC* episode broadcast was Season 11's Episode 24, "Chicago Shoe Exchange," which aired on June 9, 1997. In this episode, Kelly takes lessons in massage therapy and tries to apply those lessons to Bud. As one might imagine, things go horribly wrong for poor Bud. He ends up paralyzed! Kelly, Peg, and Jefferson take him to a mall in hopes a chiropractor can fix him. Peg refuses to pay when seeing the chiropractor's prices. Kelly and Jefferson put Bud in a tanning bed and leave him there so long he is burned. Al wants to get an expensive Swedish massage chair into the shoe store. He ends up bartering the shoes away, along with many other items, for that massage chair. Among the things that end up in the shoe store is a live chimpanzee. Al finds out Gary is coming for a visit so he and Griff scramble to get the extraneous items out and the shoes back. They forget about the chimp and the episode ends with Gary running away from the diapered animal.

END OF A SHOW, END OF AN ERA

MWC **HAD WELL OUTLASTED** the average sitcom. Christina Applegate and David Faustino had gone from children to young adults while playing Kelly and Bud, and the series helped put FOX on the map as a network. It had garnered seven Emmy nominations but no wins. It had also been nominated several times for Golden Globe Awards, without enjoying a victory. It seems likely the nominations reflect the humor and originality of the program while the lack of victories reflects its lowbrow orientation.

However, as noted, after so many years, it had pretty much exhausted the comic possibilities inherent in the characters and situations as given. The jokes had become repetitive and, to some extent, even strained. The sitcom's ratings, which had enjoyed such a hearty and welcome spike after Rakolta's campaign against the show, were sagging. After the May 6, 1997 episode aired, FOX decided it was time to cancel the long-running series.

FOX did not immediately notify the cast. Applegate recalled learning of the show's cancellation from a couple of friends. O'Neill was on vacation when he was told by a couple staying nearby that they had read in a newspaper about *MWC*'s cancellation. He appreciated their telling him about it and bought them a meal to show his gratitude.

The *Internet Movie Database* reports that Ed O'Neill has said that when he found out the show was canceled, "He talked to a FOX executive about making an episode to finish the show." He suggested an episode in which the Bundys won the lottery only to be "demolished by a tornado during their celebration."

It is good that O'Neill's idea for a final episode never came to fruition. It is unlikely viewers wanted to see the Bundys get killed. For all their faults they were likable characters, and such an episode would have left a bad taste.

Al and Peg were often at odds but ultimately bonded together by lasting love.

MWC had made history during its eleven years. According to E. E. Bell, "Katey Sagal once said to me, 'We started out as just a bunch of actors happy to get work and maybe do a season or two of this bent little show.'" However, the upshot, Bell elaborates, was great as *MWC* "went on to rewrite the face of TV comedy as the first dysfunctional family who really loved each other. Now that is the standard."

Faustino observes, "The Bundys were a family of exaggerated dysfunction. They weren't educated people, they didn't come from money, and they were more along the lines of white trash."

While the family boasted an in-your-face dysfunctionality, the Bundy family was never without a redeeming sense of love and loyalty. Al made fun of Kelly's stupidity but he also lovingly called her "Pumpkin" and was ready to beat up a man who insulted her. Bud and Kelly were often at each other's throats but let someone outside the family ridicule one of them and the other raced to the defense. Al ridiculed Peg's laziness and Peg blasted Al's sexual and financial failures, but neither ever cheated on the other. Peg relished watching male strippers at a place called Troy's and Al made frequent ogling trips to a "nudie bar," but their ultimate loyalties were ironclad. Dan Tullis Jr. believes the show's popularity lay in the way in which its basic themes spoke powerfully to a large segment of the public. "I think the show's success came from an identifiability by the audience," he states. "We all recognized the frustration of working hard and getting little in return, spiritually and mentally. Some people told me they've known people like the various characters. Money is always a problem. Relationships that seemed great at first but settled into okay or mediocrity but [we are] too comfortable to go elsewhere." Tullis also remarks on the ultimate loyalty that characterized the family: "Al and Peggy never had affairs and despite everything loved each other and the kids."

Good writing, good acting, and good all-around crafting helped make *MWC* the success that it was. Tullis comments, "The writing on that show (for Officer Dan, and let's face it, everyone) was so easy to perform I always looked forward to being on the show." As an actor, Tullis sometimes found himself torn by different commitments but tried to make time for *MWC*. "The most difficult thing was when I was in Toronto and Vancouver doing the musical *Show Boat* and they wrote me in," he recalls. "I had to fly back to L.A. on Thursday for a Friday night shoot and back North for Saturday matinees. Everyone else started on Monday. Luckily, the writing was an easy delivery."

Tullis believes that another measure of the show's success is the way it was enjoyed by people outside the country in which it originated. "I was told by a bellman in Bali that it was his favorite show," the actor remarks. "Customs in Amsterdam recognized me and talked about how much they loved the show. I heard it was #1 in Peru, Columbia, and Ecuador. Australia played it from beginning to end and started over. A former high school classmate of mine told me once that while he was going through a life-threatening disease and painful treatment he would tune in to reruns and laugh through the pain. He thanked us for the help. It is what we hope to do in entertainment, make a difference for the positive. It plays internationally, still. And it is just plain funny. All the time."

AL VS. MARCY

MUCH OF THE MOST ROLLICKING HUMOR in the show came out of the enmity between Al and next-door neighbor, Marcy. For example, in one episode Al and Peg discuss their plan to forge dental reports for their kids. Steve Rhoades points out, "Doesn't anyone know this is against the law?" Al answers, "So is dressing up a chicken and calling it your wife."

In truly inspired physical comedy, Amanda Bearse plays into Al's insult by putting her hands at her sides, elbows out, and shaking her head as she jerks up and down protesting, "I am not a chicken! Why does he keep calling me a chicken?"

During the show's run, Al made a multitude of chicken insults. He once sneeringly suggested, "Why don't you just pluck-pluck-pluck on out of here?" Seeing Marcy carrying a chicken for supper, Al congratulates her and remarks that he did not know she was "expecting." On one occasion, Al hears a chicken clucking. He says, "Marcy?" When *Psycho Dad* is canceled, Al says the person behind it is, "Marcy D'Arcy, chicken at large."

Al also often cruelly teases her about being small-breasted. One time he mentions that a difference between the two of them is that if he leans forward and pushes his chest together, he looks like he has breasts. In one such exchange, she taunts that she does not have to tell him "how much easier it is to lug around small things," a remark suggesting his penis is small.

Related to the jokes about her flat chest are jokes suggesting she looks more male than female. On a Christmastime episode, Marcy declares that she will win the neighborhood-decorating contest. "What are you going to do, Marcy, stand outside and be the little drummer boy?" Al asks.

After the show went off the air, O'Neill admitted in an interview that, in real life, he did not get along well with Amanda Bearse. It is quite possible that his real-life dislike for her was a plus for the program because it made their comically bitter banter all the more credible.

There are significant cinematic precedents for this. For example, in the 1933 film *Dinner at Eight*, Jean Harlow and Wallace Beery, known for their personal antagonism, were cast as a squabbling married couple in the belief that their dislike of each other would heighten the tension between the screen characters they played. In the 1962 film *Whatever Happened To Baby Jane?*, Bette Davis and Joan Crawford, real-life rivals who despised each other, were cast as quarreling sisters. There are reports that Crawford insisted a mannequin be used in the scene in which Davis's character repeatedly kicks Crawford's character because Crawford could not trust enemy Davis to fake the kicks.

Thus, while it must be seen as unfortunate that O'Neill and Bearse disliked each other, the *MWC* audience may have benefited from it.

THE LOST EPISODE IS AIRED

About five years after *MWC* went off the air—and well over a decade after it had first been scheduled to air—American viewers first got a chance to see the episode that had been long called "The Lost Episode," since FOX did not want to put this episode on while Terry Rakolta's anti-*MWC* campaign was still going strong. Even when finally aired, a brief exchange filmed in the original was edited out. That exchange was not especially sexy, but was one of Marcy making distasteful threats. For example, "I'll do things to them that'll make the devil himself vomit."

"I'll See You in Court" begins with Peg yearning to spice up the marriage. Marcy confides in her that she and Steve get horny with a change of scenery. A good place to have hot sex with the spouse, Marcy elaborates, is the Hop-On-Inn. Peg talks Al into taking a trip to this establishment. The couple turns on the TV and sees a sex video. They are soon perplexed by what they are watching and realize that they are watching Steve and Marcy having sex!

Happy to embarrass their often-arrogant neighbors, the Bundys gleefully inform the Rhoades that the Hop-On-Inn videotaped their marital lovemaking for posterity.

But Bundy glee curdles into shame when the Rhoades point out that the Hop-On-Inn probably also taped *their* relations!

Al and Marcy want to commit violence against the Hop-On-Inn violators in retaliation. Steve and Peg prefer the all-American lawsuit and the money it can bring.

Steve acts as the attorney for he and Marcy and Al and Peg. In his opening statement, he veers away from the spicy facts of the case to a civics lesson in American rights and privacy that soon has both court stenographer and judge falling asleep.

To prove his case, Steve intends to show Exhibit A, which is the tape of he and Marcy, and Exhibit B, the tape of Al and Peg.

However, Marcy is understandably mortified at the idea of her most intimate moments being viewed in open court. She expresses horror that he will show the tape of the lovemaking in court. He points out they stand to win as much as a million dollars. "Doesn't my honor mean more to you than a million dollars?" she plaintively asks.

It is immediately apparent that Steve will take the money. However, this exchange underlines again the instability that the program showed in the depiction of Marcy's personality, veering between prim and radical, between Democrat and Republican, between feminine and butch.

The clock shows the hour hand happily and quickly going around a clock's face four times, indicating that Steve and Marcy enjoyed sex for four hours! This results in the courtroom breaking out into applause.

Exhibit B of the Bundys is shown and the clock appears to show that the event lasted less than one minute!

The defense calls Marcy to the stand. In an effort to show that she willingly allowed herself to be filmed having sex, the attorney brings out that she wears crotch-less underpants and plays sex games with handcuffs.

When Peg is called to the stand, the defense suggests that no sex took place. How can something that lasted less than a minute deserve to be called sex? Peg answers, "Is a crumb not a banquet for a starving person? Is a fig leaf not clothing for the naked?"

The jury awards $10,000 to the Rhoadeses but nothing to the Bundys.

It is all-too-likely that viewers watching the finally aired and almost legendary episode were disappointed. That this one episode had not been aired because of the Rakolta crusade and was finally aired so many years later probably led people to expect something super-titillating and absolutely "out-there." Although the episode was funny, like all *MWC* episodes, most of its "sexiest" humor was drawn from the show's standard tropes, including Marcy and Steve's highly sexual marriage and Al's legendary lack of sexual staying power; buildup can lead to letdown—as Peg well knew.

COMICAL BUT COMPASSIONATE, LIBERAL BUT CONSERVATIVE

MWC **WAS A LANDMARK PROGRAM,** and it has rightly become a classic. Its breakthroughs were many and major. The Bundy family was profoundly dysfunctional, and they were often crude and obnoxious in language and behavior. The family even committed petty crimes, especially small thefts. Al was not a fount of wisdom for his children, and frequently avoided father-child talks in favor of watching TV or just loafing. He made endless nasty remarks to fat women, other unattractive women, and next-door nemesis, Marcy. Peg could be equally crude and even raunchier. She was selfish and sarcastic. Kelly flaunted her young body in sexy clothes and juggled boyfriends. Bud was the closest thing to an intellectual that the Bundys produced, but even he was often distracted by horniness and preferred the pleasures of the flesh to those of the mind.

It should be noted that the program was oddly unfair to a sizeable group of workers, shoe salespeople. Because it was Al Bundy's job, it was depicted as the lowest, and even most shameful occupation a person could have. In reality, there is nothing horrible about the occupation of shoe salesperson. It may expose a worker to unpleasant foot odor, but it is hardly the grungiest job in the world. A bad smelling foot does not usually carry as offensive an odor as a dirty diaper or can of garbage. People who work in sewers and on farms often deal with odors far more unpleasant than foot odors. Indeed, surgeons typically deal with much that is far worse than those who sell shoes for a living. Selling shoes is an honest and completely respectable job. As Lisa Finn writes in "The Job Description of a Shoe Salesman," people who "are good at it may gain loyal customers, as well as a decent salary." Finn elaborates that "shoe salesmen often earn a salary plus commission." A man–or woman–who sells shoes need neither be disgraced nor impoverished.

Dad and daughter face off.

Of course, it was believable, and rather heartrending, that Al was disappointed at his job since, as a youth, he had dreamed of being a professional football player. Indeed, much of the comedy of *MWC* was based on disappointment and disillusion. The high point of Al's life had been in high school when he was admired for his athletic prowess and street smarts. Similarly, Peg looked back at her high school days as those when she was admired for her sexiness. Al made this point when he told her that something could "tighten more nuts than you did in high school." After years of marriage, it was believable that Al was no longer lusting after her body, even though it was still slender and shapely, as he had been when they first became a couple. The sexual frankness of the program and the overall irreverence spoke powerfully to liberal impulses and helped attract the young, "hip," urban audience FOX had targeted.

Nevertheless, it is at least arguable that *MWC* was powered by many traditional impulses. For one thing, it showcased a traditional division of gender roles in which the husband is the provider and the wife the dependent. In an era in which the media showcases women in a wide variety of roles, where women are commonly portrayed in such non-traditional jobs as lawyer and judge, doctor and detective, it was positively refreshing to see a program focus on a housewife. In a way, it was even more refreshing to see a housewife who was, at least after Season 1, not a bustling June Cleaver or Donna Reed, but endearingly lazy. The truth is that "occupation housewife" is performed in more varied styles than other jobs, and the housewife who does little housework, like the industrious and efficient housewife, is part of reality. Thus, it was nice to see that group represented on TV, especially by a character as likeable as Peg Bundy.

That being a housewife, including being a leisurely housewife, is preferred by at least some women is also a valid point *MWC* often made. As previously noted, women's libber extremists tend to work at occupations that are both creative and challenging. Like Marcy with Peg, they project their own preferences on women who prefer to financially depend on their husbands. The truth is that there may be more of interest on daytime TV shows like *Dr. Phil* and *Oprah* than there is in the average low-level job. Thus, it was entirely credible that Peg preferred staying home to standing behind a counter in a store.

In an excellent and incisive article for the right-wing magazine *National Review*, John Derbyshire wrote an article underlining *MWC*'s traditional aspects. Derbyshire says *MWC* is "one of the most conservative shows on TV." He elaborates, "Al hates his

Peg taught Kelly the traditional ideology that wives should financially depend on their husbands.

work, but he goes to work every day nonetheless. The Bundys' marriage is stale, but they stay married anyway. The kids are slaves to their own libidos, but it's hard to imagine them doing anything unkind or seriously illegal, or turning into dope addicts." The writer observes that underlying the basic set-up of the show "was the principle of *duty*." As previously noted, no matter how much Al fantasizes about a "free" life of no work and easy "babes," he returns to work to eke out a living for his family. Peg may be dissatisfied both financially and sexually with Al, but she sticks resolutely by him. The kids tease each other mercilessly but stand by each other when threatened by those outside the family.

Perhaps what ultimately made *MWC* a popular show and a classic was the wonderful blending of iconoclasm and conservatism. For all the defects one finds in most marriages, the truth is that there is unlikely to be anything that will actually replace marriage as a customary relationship. As was true for Al and Peg Bundy, the lifestyle of the vast majority of people will include marriage. While some very successful marriages will be childless, the majority of marriages will include children. *Married... with Children* is a sitcom title describing what life has been for most people throughout the human story, and what it will be for most people in the future. Such basic truths of human existence were the foundation of this show's longevity, as well as its secure status as a TV classic.

BIBLIOGRAPHY

THE AUTHOR EXTENDS a very special and warm thanks to David Garrison, Ritch Shydner, Jonathan Wolff, Steven Ritt, Scott I. Glickman, Dick Warlock, E. E. Bell, and Gary Grubbs for their assistance through agreeing to be interviewed by her.

A Day in the Life of Married With Children. https://www.youtube.com/watch?v=A5nE89M7HIw

"All in the Family." *Married with Children.* Internet Movie Database. http://www.imdb.com/title/tt0642218

Byrd, Veronica and Gene Seymour. "Has 'Married… With Children' been muzzled?" *Entertainment Weekly.* Feb. 16, 1990.

"Christina Applegate." Internet Movie Database. http://www.imdb.com/name/nm0000775/?ref_=fn_al_nm_1

"David Faustino." Internet Movie Database. http://www.imdb.com/name/nm0004910/?ref_=fn_al_nm_1

Derbyshire, John. "Children of a Conservative God." *National Review.* Feb. 21, 2003.

"Ed O'Neill." Internet Movie Database. http://www.imdb.com/name/nm0642145/?ref_=nv_sr_1

"Her Cups Runneth Over." *Married with Children.* http://www.imdb.com/title/tt0642285/?ref_=fn_al_tt_1

"He Thought He Could." *Married with Children*. Internet Movie Database. http://www.imdb.com/title/tt0642284/?ref_=fn_al_tt_1

"I'll See You in Court" (0308). Hypertext Program Guide. Bundyology. http://www.bundyology.com/hpg/308.html

"I'll See You in Court." *Married with Children*. Internet Movie Database. http://www.imdb.com/title/tt0642298/?ref_=fn_al_tt_1

"Katey Sagal." Internet Movie Database. http://www.imdb.com/name/nm0005408/?ref_=fn_al_nm_1

Married with Children (1987-1997). Awards. http://www.imdb.com/title/tt0092400/awards?ref_=tt_ql_op_1

Married with Children (1987-1997). http://www.imdb.com/title/tt0092400/?ref_=ttep_ep_tt

Married with Children Documentary. https://www.youtube.com/watch?v=SroICnksANA

Married with Children. Episode List. Season 1. Internet Movie Database. http://www.imdb.com/title/tt0092400/episodes?season=1

Married with Children. Episode List. Season 2. Internet Movie Database. http://www.imdb.com/title/tt0092400/episodes?season=2

Married with Children. Episode List. Season 3. Internet Movie Database. http://www.imdb.com/title/tt0092400/episodes?season=3

Married with Children. Episode List. Season 4. Internet Movie Database. http://www.imdb.com/title/tt0092400/episodes?season=4

Married with Children. Episode List. Season 5. Internet Movie Database. http://www.imdb.com/title/tt0092400/episodes?season=5

Married with Children. Episode List. Season 6. Internet Movie Database. http://www.imdb.com/title/tt0092400/episodes?season=6

Married with Children. Episode List. Season 7. Internet Movie Database. http://www.imdb.com/title/tt0092400/episodes?season=7

Married with Children. Episode List. Season 8. Internet Movie Database. http://www.imdb.com/title/tt0092400/episodes?season=8

Married with Children. Episode List. Season 9. Internet Movie Database. http://www.imdb.com/title/tt0092400/episodes?season=9

Married with Children. Episode List. Season 10. Internet Movie Database. http://www.imdb.com/title/tt0092400/episodes?season=10

Married with Children. Episode List. Season 11. Internet Movie Database. http://www.imdb.com/title/tt0092400/episodes?season=11

Married with Children (1987-1997) Full Cast & Crew. Internet Movie Database. http://www.imdb.com/title/tt0092400/fullcredits

Married with Children MTV Backstage 1992. https://www.youtube.com/watch?v=jfASRheHccE

Married with Children Reunion. https://www.youtube.com/watch?v=ZxkGW3eb_RA

Married with Children (1987-1997). Trivia. http://www.imdb.com/title/tt0092400/trivia?ref_=tt_ql_2

Mullins, Jenna. "19 Things You Probably Didn't Know About *Married... with Children*." E News. Nov. 20, 2015. http://www.eonline.com/news/717462/19-things-you-probably-didn-t-know-about-married-with-children

"NO MA'AM." Bundyology. http://www.bundyology.com/nomaam.html

Pilot. *Married with Children*. http://www.imdb.com/title/tt0642348/?ref_=ttep_ep2

Shydner, Ritch. *Kicking Through The Ashes—My Life As A Stand-up in The 1980s Boom*. CreateSpace Independent Publishing Platform. 2016.

"Studios." Bundyology. Feb. 10, 2005. http://www.bundyology.com/studios.html

"Terry Rakolta's Fight against Married… with Children." Bundyology. http://www.bundyology.com/rakolta.html

APPENDIX OF MARRIED... WITH CHILDREN EPISODES

SEASON 1

1. April 5, 1987. Pilot
Al has a chance to go to a basketball game, but Peg wants him home to meet new neighbors. Peg says, "The bank account is in both our names. The credit cards are in both our names. And the stores are still open." Al stays home, and he and Peg meet Marcy and Steve Rhoades.

2. April 12, 1987. "Thinnergy"
Marcy suggests Peg go on a new diet. Al is upset by it but agrees to go on it himself in the hopes that they will go off it together.

3. April 19, 1987. "But I Didn't Shoot the Deputy"
After several neighborhood burglaries, Al decides to buy a firearm while the Rhoadeses buy a guard dog—which Al accidentally shoots.

4. April 26, 1987. "Whose Room Is It Anyway?"
The Rhoadeses get a tax refund, and both want to build a new room. Steve wants a billiards room and Marcy wants an exercise room. Al urges Steve to insist on his preference while Peg urges Marcy to be equally insistent on hers, and complications ensue.

5. May 3, 1987. "Have You Driven A Ford Lately?"
Al and Steve buy an old car and spend so much time fixing it up that their wives feel neglected.

6. **May 10, 1987. "Sixteen Years and What Do You Get?"**
   It is the Bundys 16th anniversary. When Al tries to buy Peg a gift, his credit card is declined.

7. **May 17, 1987. "Married… Without Children"**
   Al and Peggy go for a vacation sans Kelly and Bud. Steve and Marcy agree to watch the kids and Buck.

8. **May 24, 1987. "The Poker Game"**
   Al wins $300 from Steve in a poker game and Steve is terrified about Marcy learning of the loss.

9. **May 31, 1987. "Peggy Sue Got Work"**
   Marcy insists Peg get a job in a store selling clocks. Peg chafes at this "liberation" and yearns for the couch and daytime T.V.

10. **June 7, 1987. "Al Loses His Cherry"**
    Al visits coworker Luke's bachelor pad. Al (just barely) avoids the temptation to cheat with a swinging young lady.

11. **June 14, 1987. "Nightmare on Al's Street"**
    Despite her disdain for Al, Marcy begins to have romantic and sexual dreams about him.

12. **June 21, 1987. "Where's the Boss?"**
    Al hears that the owner of the shoe store at which he works came close to dying, and Al becomes obsessed with why the owner has never visited the store.

13. **June 28, 1987. "Johnny Be Gone"**
    The Bundys learn that their favorite hamburger joint is going to close.

SEASON 2

1. **Sept. 27, 1987. "Poppy's by the Tree, Pt. 1"**
   The Bundys vacation in Dumpwater, Florida. They do not realize that the hotel's tourists are the targets of a serial murderer.

2. Sept. 27, 1987. "Poppy's by the Tree, Pt. 2"
The serial murderer takes Peg hostage and threatens to axe her to death.

3. Oct. 4, 1987. "If I Were A Rich Man"
Al visits Steve at the bank at which he is employed. Later, it is reported that $1 million is missing from the bank. Peg and the kids, as well as Steve, think Al stole it despite his denials.

4. Oct. 11, 1987. "Buck Can Do It"
Buck has been siring so many puppies that the decision is made to neuter him. Al has a bizarre fantasy in which Buck reads the riot act to him about this decision.

5. Oct. 18, 1987. "Girls Just Wanna Have Fun, Pt. 1"
Al and Steve ogle a pretty woman fixing the Bundy refrigerator. To get back, Marcy agrees to accompany Peg to a strip club featuring male strippers and catering to a female audience.

6. Oct. 18, 1987. "Girls Just Wanna Have Fun, Pt. 2"
Marcy is terrified when she realizes that she has lost her wedding ring because it slipped down the pants of a male stripper when she tipped him.

7. Oct. 25, 1987. "For Whom the Bell Tolls"
Al will not pay for a long-distance phone call and the Bundys lose phone service. He is also troubled by a streetlight that keeps him awake.

8. Nov. 1, 1987. "Born to Walk"
Kelly passes the test for a driver's license and Al fails.

9. Nov. 8, 1987. "Alley of the Dolls"
The Bundys get into a fiercely competitive bowling match with a family that includes a woman who was a high school rival to Peg.

10. Nov. 15, 1987. "The Razor's Edge"
After spending a week away from Marcy on a rafting trip, Steve has grown a beard. Marcy's wants to cut it off; Al urges Steve to keep it.

11. **Nov. 22, 1987. "How Do You Spell Revenge?"**
    Al, Peg, and Bud are in a shopping mall softball team. Al tells Peg she must improve her game or she is off the team.

12. **Dec. 6, 1987. "Earth Angel"**
    Pretty Tiffany gets all the neighborhood men aroused. Most of the wives are happy because the hubbies "bring it home," but Marcy is strongly displeased to know Steve is ogling another woman.

13. **Dec. 20, 1987. "You Better Watch Out"**
    The Bundy family is celebrating Christmas. A mall has a Santa Claus who ends up parachuting into the Bundy backyard.

14. **Jan. 10, 1988. "Guys and Dolls"**
    Al and Steve sell an old Barbie doll of Marcy's. When Steve learns how much that doll means to Marcy, he must get it back.

15. **Jan. 24, 1988. "Build A Better Mousetrap"**
    There is a rat in the Bundy house and Al is determined to slay the creature.

17. **Feb. 7, 1988. "Master the Possibilities"**
    A credit card in Buck's name is mailed to the Bundy residence. Believing they cannot be held responsible for the card, Al and Peg enjoy a spending spree.

18. **Feb. 14, 1988. "Peggy Love Al—Yeah, Yeah, Yeah"**
    It is Valentine's Day. Kelly receives a multitude of valentines, Bud pines for a valentine, and Peg yearns for Al to reaffirm his love.

19. **Feb. 21, 1988. "The Great Escape"**
    Because the Bundy residence has been found to be infested with termites, the entire family takes refuge in the shoe store.

20. **Feb. 28, 1988. "Im-Po-Dent"**
    Marcy crashes Steve's car; Steve has sexual difficulties.

21. **Mar. 6, 1988. "Just Married... With Children"**
    Peg and Al apply to be guests on a T.V. game show in which contestants

must endure physical torture from their spouses.

22. Mar. 13, 1988. "Father Lode"
Al gets a big win at the racetrack but does not want his family to know.

23. May 1, 1988. "All in the Family"
Al wants to enjoy a weekend in which he can watch his favorite John Wayne film, *Hondo*, but Al finds his weekend ruined by a visit from Peg's mom, two uncles, and triplet aunts.

SEASON 3

1. Nov. 6, 1988. "He Thought He Could"
Al needs to return a library book that is more than a decade overdue. Flashback to a little Al Bundy with hand down pants.

2. Nov. 20, 1988. "I'm Going to Sweatland"
Al stains a shirt with sweat that appears to be a silhouette of Elvis Presley.

3. Nov. 27, 1988. "Poke High"
A young football player might break two records set at Polk High by Al.

4. Dec. 11, 1988. "The Camping Show"
The Bundys and Rhoadeses head to a cabin in the woods for a fun vacation. Peg, Kelly, and Marcy get their menstrual periods at the same time and a bear makes a car attack.

5. Jan. 8, 1989. "A Dump of My Own"
The upstairs toilet has repeatedly flooded so Al wants to build a spare bathroom.

6. Jan. 15, 1989. "Her Cups Runneth Over"
Peg learns her favorite bra model has ceased production. Al goes to a faraway lingerie store to get a bra of her preferred type. This was a pivotal episode: Terry Rakolta began her anti-*MWC* campaign after watching it.

7. **Jan. 29, 1989. "The Bald and the Beautiful"**
   Steve is distressed at the prospect of losing his hair. He brings Al to a meeting of Bald American Dudes (BAD).

8. **Feb. 5, 1989. "The Gypsy Cried"**
   A fortune teller predicts good fortune for the Bundys and Steve Rhoades, but doom for Marcy.

9. **Feb. 12, 1989. "Requiem for a Dead Barber"**
   Al's longtime barber dies and Al goes to a hair salon. At the hair salon, he gets a hairstyle Bud identifies as having "That no closet can hold me look." His buddies go to the same hair salon and receive similar looks.

10. **Feb. 19, 1989. "Eatin' Out"**
    Al gets an inheritance windfall of $237. The family splurges at a fancy restaurant—then Al sees he forgot to bring the check!

11. **Feb. 26, 1989. "My Mom, the Mom"**
    Kelly's high school is holding a career day that Peg attends. Soon Peg, as housewife, is getting more attention from the young ladies than the judge and astronaut.

12. **Mar. 18, 1989. "Can't Dance, Don't Ask Me"**
    Kelly has a hassle at school. She must appear in a school performance as a tap dancer or be expelled.

13. **Apr. 2, 1989. "A Three Job, No Income Family"**
    Al nags Peg to contribute to the household income. She gets a job selling cosmetics, but there is a comical twist to this attempt to earn that leaves the family in the financial lurch.

14. **Mar. 25, 1989. "The Harder They Fall"**
    Steve drives Peg back from a store. Someone cuts Steve off in traffic and Peg gives that driver "the finger." Steve fears retaliation after being followed home by that driver.

15. **Apr. 9, 1989. "The House That Peg Lost"**
    Steve and Marcy ask the Bundys to watch their house while they leave for the day. The Rhoadeses come home to find a hole where

their house stood!

16. Apr. 23, 1989. "Married… with Prom Queen, Pt. 1"
Peg and Al attend a Polk High School Reunion. Peg and an old high school rival vie for "Reunion Queen" title.

17. Apr. 30, 1989. "Married… with Prom Queen, Pt. 2"
The summing up of the previously mentioned rivalry.

18. May 7, 1989. "The Dateless Amigo"
Bud desperately wants a date but tries to settle for a mannequin.

19. May 4, 1989. "The Computer Store"
The Bundys buy a computer that ends up serving as a hat rack. However, the computer "talks" to Al.

20. May 21, 1989. "Life's A Beach"
The Bundys at the beach.

21. Aug. 27, 1989. "Here's Looking at You, Kid"
A serial peeper is loose in the neighborhood and Peg wonders why he has not tried to look at her.

SEASON 4

1. Sept. 3, 1989. "Hot Off the Grill"
On Labor Day, usual Bundy roles are reversed as Al takes it easy and Peg prepares the barbecue. The gross-out discovery is that the ashes of Marcy's dead aunt were in the grill!

2. Sept 10, 1989. "Dead Men Don't do Aerobics"
A TV aerobics instructor tries to get the Bundys to exercise but ends up following their sedentary lifestyle and dying of a heart attack.

3. Sept. 24, 1989. "Buck Saves the Day"
Al, Steve, Bud, and a group of boys go camping. They try to get Buck to return home with a note in his mouth so the women will come to the campsite for a rescue.

4. Oct. 1, 1989. "Tooth or Consequences"
   Al gets a toothache. He goes to a dentist who seems more interested in his sexy dental assistant than his work.

5. Oct. 8, 1989. "He Ain't Much but He's Mine"
   Al starts coming home late and Peg suspects cheating.

6. Oct. 29, 1989. "Fair Exchange"
   The Bundys host a pretty French foreign exchange student.

7. Nov. 5, 1989. "Desperately Seeking Miss October"
   Al is devastated to find out that Peg sold his *Playboy* collection. The ghost of Al's dad pays a visit to Al.

8. Nov. 12, 1989. "976-SHOE"
   Al borrows money through Steve's bank to set up a hotline for people who have questions about shoes. As might be imagined, this shoe hotline is hardly a big hit with the public.

9. Nov. 19, 1989. "Oh, What A Feeling"
   The Dodge conks out and Al searches for an affordable vehicle.

10. Nov. 26, 1989. "At the Zoo"
    An unemployed Steve spends his time visiting the zoo instead of looking for work, to Marcy's disgust.

11. Dec. 17, 1989. "It's a Bundyful Life, Pt. 1"
    Al fails to get to the bank in time to provide his family with Christmas presents.

12. Dec.17, 1989. "It's a Bundyful Life, Pt. 2"
    A guardian angel shows Al how nice life would have been if he had never been born. To the angel's surprise, it makes Al want to live so he can make his family miserable.

13. Jan. 7, 1990. "Who'll Stop the Rain"
    Al will not call in a repairperson and insists on fixing the house's leaking roof himself despite his falls off that roof.

14. **Jan. 14, 1990. "A Taxing Audit"**
Al faces an IRS audit because of Peg's attempt to pull the wool over the IRS's eyes. Al wants to sell Peg's red hair to pay what is owed.

15. **Feb. 4, 1990. "Rock and Roll Girl"**
Al challenges the family to help him bring in money. Kelly gets a job in a rock video.

16. **Feb. 11, 1990. "You Gotta Know When to Hold 'Em, Pt. 1"**
Steve leaves Marcy. To lift Marcy's spirits, Peg takes her to Las Vegas.

17. **Feb. 18, 1990. "You Gotta Know When to Fold 'Em, Pt. 2"**
Al and the kids go to Las Vegas where they find that Peg and Marcy are broke.

18. **Feb. 25, 1990. "What Goes Around Comes Around"**
Bud hopes to make up with a girl who bullied him in elementary school.

19. **Mar. 25, 1990. "Peggy Turns 300"**
It is Peg's birthday. She hopes to show off at a bowling alley and show up an old high school rival.

20. **Apr. 15, 1990. "Peggy Made a Little Lamb"**
After finding out she never really got her high school diploma, Peg takes a home economics course to finally get that diploma.

21. **Apr. 29, 1990. "Rain Girl"**
Kelly gets a chance to be a TV weather reporter, but reading the teleprompter is her downfall.

22. **May 6, 1990. "The Agony of De-Feet"**
Nightmares of ugly feet plague Al, who is then chosen to be a judge in a contest in which the judges look only at feet!

23. **May 13, 1990. "Yard Sale"**
Over Peg's protests, Al has a yard sale to try to sell off the odd merchandise that Peg has purchased at other yard sales.

SEASON 5

1. Sept. 23, 1990. "We'll Follow the Sun"
The Bundys take a Labor Day weekend vacation and spend much of it stuck in traffic.

2. Sept. 30, 1990. "Al… with Kelly"
Al and Kelly pretend they are sick to avoid accompanying Peg and Bud to Wanker County. Things go awry for Al when Kelly really gets sick.

3. Oct. 7, 1990 . "Sue Casa, His Casa"
Bud gets a driver's license and soon gets into a fender bender with a Mercedes. The other party sues and the Bundys fake injuries and counter sue.

4. Oct. 14, 1990. "The Unnatural"
The neighborhood softball team replaces Al with a pro player—who is soon injured. The team must ask Al to return.

5. Oct. 21, 1990. "Dance Show"
Peg goes out dancing with Marcy. Peg becomes entranced with a man named Andy. A man appears on the doorstep when Al is home alone to inform Al, "Your wife has been seeing my husband."

6. Oct. 28, 1990. "Kelly Bounces Back"
Kelly plans to perform "The Bundy Bounce" when she auditions to become spokesperson for a car, but sees at the audition that another model has stolen her idea.

7. Nov. 4, 1990. "Married… with Aliens"
Al begins seeing six little green aliens. No one else sees them so he takes photographs that he hopes will make him wealthy.

8. Nov. 11, 1990. "Wabbit Season"
Al tries to grow a vegetable garden but a persistent rabbit keeps eating what Al plants.

Appendix of *Married... With Children* Episodes • 97

9. Nov. 18, 1990. "Do Ya Think I'm Sexy"
Neighborhood women start ogling Al and he begins trying to present himself as an elegant man about town.

10. Nov. 25, 1990. "One Down, Two to Go"
Al kicks one of Kelly's boyfriends out of the house. Kelly decides to get her own apartment.

11. Dec. 16, 1990. "And Baby Makes Money"
An uncle of Al's dies. In his will, he leaves half a million dollars to the first Bundy who can produce a baby boy within wedlock that will be named after the deceased.

12. Jan. 6, 1991. "Married... with Who"
Marcy passes out after a wild party at a bankers' convention. When she awakens, she realizes she is now Marcy D'Arcy, wife of handsome hunk Jefferson.

13. Feb. 3, 1991. "The Godfather"
Kelly dates a member of the city council. Through that relationship, Al gains power in the neighborhood and begins presenting himself as a kind of Don Corleone.

14. Feb. 17, 1991. "A Man's Castle"
Peg takes an interior decorating class. Al is outraged when he sees how she has "beautified" his spare bathroom.

15. Feb. 24, 1991. "All-Nite Security Dude"
Laid off from the shoe store, Al works as a night security guard at Polk High. An old school rival steals Al's prized trophy, leading the two into a battle.

16. Mar. 17, 1991. "Oldies but Young 'Uns"
A tune on the radio, the name of which Al does not know, begins to haunt him. He feels like he *must* track down a record with that song.

17. Mar. 24, 1991. "Weenie Tot Lovers & Other Strangers"
Kelly competes to become Miss Weenie Tot. Since Weenie Tots are a favorite food of Al's, he is delighted when she wins.

18. Mar. 31, 1991. "Kids! Wadaya Gonna Do?"
Kelly babysits a rambunctious bunch of seven children.

19. Apr. 7, 1991. "Top of the Heap"
About Al's friend and the friend's son. Pilot for short-lived TV show *Top of the Heap.*

20. Apr. 14, 1991. "You Better Shop Around, Pt. 1"
Without an air conditioner, the Bundys take refuge in the neighborhood supermarket. Told to buy something or get out, Al cuts in front of Marcy, making him the winner of a $1,000 shopping spree.

21. Apr. 26, 1991. "You Better Shop Around, Pt. 2"
Marcy protests that Al cannot be the true winner since he cut in front of her. The store manager says the Bundys and D'Arcys may compete against each other to find who should be the shopping spree winner.

22. Apr. 28, 1991. "Route 666, Pt. 1"
The Bundys are heading for a "Shoe Convention" when their car breaks down in rural Lucifer, New Mexico. They think they can get rich by searching for gold

23. May 5, 1991. "Route 666, Pt. 2"
The Bundys and the D'Arcys think they are going to get wealthy from the gold in their bags, but they find a problem.

24. May 19, 1991. "Buck the Stud"
A man offers Al a large payment if Buck breeds with the man's female dog.

SEASON 6

1. Sept. 8, 1991. "She's Having a Baby, Pt. 1"
Marcy announces she is having a baby. Al ribs Jefferson before learning that Peg is also pregnant.

2. Sept. 15, 1991. "She's Having a Baby, Pt. 2"
Al and Jefferson are tempted to run out on their pregnant wives, but both are ultimately loyal and return home.

3. Sept. 22, 1991. "If Al Had a Hammer"
Al discovers a hammer that once belonged to his dad. Al decides to make the garage into his own private room.

4. Sept. 29, 1991. "Cheese, Cues, and Blood"
Al learns Kelly is earning money during the evenings and suspects sex work but learns she is a pool shark.

5. Oct. 6, 1991 . "Lookin' for a Desk in All the Wrong Places"
Marcy learned that Jefferson auctioned off her precious childhood desk. With Peg in tow, Marcy searches desperately for the item.

6. Oct. 13, 1991. "Buck Has a Belly Ache"
Peg is jealous that a listless Buck is getting more attention than pregnant Peg.

7. Oct. 27, 1991. "If I Could See Me Now"
The kids try to convince Al that he should get eyeglasses.

8. Nov. 6, 1991. "God's Shoes"
Al has a fall that knocks him unconscious. When he awakens, he is convinced he saw God's shoes and must bring similar shoes to the world.

9. Nov. 10, 1991. "Kelly Does Hollywood, Pt. 1"
Kelly gets her own TV talk show, "Vital Social Issues N' Stuff with Kelly."

10. Nov. 17, 1991. "Kelly Does Hollywood, Pt. 2"
The bigwigs at the TV network insist Kelly change the type of show of which she is hostess.

11. Nov. 24, 1991. "Al Bundy, Shoe Dick"
Al is a detective who solves a sensational case. Then he awakens to realize that it is a dream. He learns that Peg's pregnancy and Marcy's pregnancy were also just dreams.

12. Dec. 1, 1991. "So This is How Sinatra Felt"
A pretty "shoe groupie" pursues Al.

13. Dec. 22, 1991. "I Who Have Nothing"
Al wants the game ball he long ago gave away to a high school girlfriend.

14. Jan. 5, 1992. "The Mystery of Skull Island"
Bud appears as rapper "Grandmaster B." Peg invites Al, along with Marcy and Jefferson, to play a board game called "Ethical Dilemma."

15. Jan. 19, 1992. "Just Shoe It"
Al appears in a TV commercial for an athletic shoe brand. He ends up pummeled by Ed "Too Tall" Jones, Sugar Ray Leonard, and Steve Carlton.

16. Feb. 9, 1992. "Rites of Passage"
For Bud's 18th birthday, Peg and others plan a party complete with clown. Al wants to take Bud to his first trip to The Nudie Bar.

17. Feb. 16, 1992. "The Egg and I"
Steve is on the run from his forest ranger job because he has stolen a rare bird's egg. He intends to reclaim Marcy, unaware she is wed to another man.

18. Feb. 23, 1992. "My Dinner with Anthrax"
Kelly and Bud win a contest, the prize of which is a house party with the metal band Anthrax. To have the band over, the kids need to get their parents out of the house.

19. Mar. 1, 1992. "Psychic Avengers"
Al joins Jefferson in a psychic phone line scam.

20. Mar. 22, 1992. "High I.Q."
Kelly is proud when she is invited to a party of a club of people known for high intelligence. However, Bud tells her there is a reason behind the invitation that is anything but flattering.

21. Apr. 5, 1992. "Teacher Pets"
Bud is sure his substitute teacher has a crush on him. The teacher leaves. Will the next teacher have amorous desires for Bud?

Appendix of *Married... With Children* Episodes • 101

22. Apr. 19, 1992. "The Goodbye Girl"
Kelly gets a job as a greeter at a theme park. She is soon sick of telling everyone "goodbye." She is re-assigned to become "The Verminator."

23. Apr. 26, 1992. "The Gas Station Show"
Unable to pay his gas station bill, Al must work off what he owes wearing a uniform with the name "Habib" stitched on it.

24. May 3, 1992. "England Show, Pt. 1"
In Lower Uncton, England, 1652, an infuriated witch places a curse on Seamus McBundy and all his male descendants. Lower Uncton itself bears the burden of darkness because of the witch's curse. In the 1992 present, Lower Uncton is still ever in darkness. The people of the cursed town seek to find the last living male Bundys and kill them to lift the curse.

25. May 10, 1992. "England Show, Pt. 2"
The Bundys vacation in England. The Lower Uncton people take them into the town where they plan to hang Al and Bud.

26. May 17, 1992. "England Show, Pt. 3"
Al challenges Lower Uncton's Igor to a joust so Al can save his own life as well as Bud's. Igor is an experienced athlete but Al has a special weapon that can drive a horse almost to madness.

SEASON 7

1. Sept. 13, 1992. "Magnificent Seven"
Peg's cousin Zemus and his wife visit the Bundys. When the couple leave, their young son Seven stays.

2. Sept. 20, 1992. "T-R-A Something-Something Spells Tramp"
For once, everyone seems to enjoy satisfying romantic encounters except Kelly.

3. Sept. 27, 1992. "Every Bundy Has a Birthday"
Peg cannot find anyone who knows Seven's date of birth. She wants to celebrate his birthday, so she "gives" him Al's birthday.

4. Oct. 4, 1992. "Al on the Rocks"
Bundy debts lead Al to take a moonlighting job as a bartender in a bar catering to women in which the male bartender is expected to be shirtless. Jefferson covers for Al once and ends up taking Al's job.

5. Oct. 11, 1992. "What I did for Love"
Peg realizes that the only way to get Al to have sex is to cook for him, so she makes that supreme sacrifice.

6. Oct. 25, 1992. "Frat Chance"
Bud begins his own fraternity, "Alpha Gunna Get Em."

7. Nov. 1, 1992. "The Chicago Wine Party"
On election day, the Bundys are upset when a new 2-cent beer tax passes.

8. Nov. 8, 1992. "Kelly Doesn't Live Here Anymore"
Peg is upset that Kelly plans to work as Peg wants her daughter to follow the Wanker tradition of women living lives of leisure. Kelly becomes a waitress in a greasy spoon and reminds Peg of Al.

9. Nov. 15, 1992. "Rock of Ages"
Al wins a shoe selling contest. The prize is a trip to Hawaii. On the way, the Bundys travel to Chicago's O'Hare Airport where he pretends to be an old rocker named Axel Bundy and gets to be around a group of famous rockers.

10. Nov. 22, 1992. "Death of a Shoe Salesman"
Al buys a graveyard plot next to his favorite film character. But Peg is insistent that she be buried next to Al.

11. Dec. 13, 1992. "The Old College Try"
Al and Peg take Bud's college grant money and go on a shopping spree.

12. Dec. 20, 1992. "Christmas"
To buy Christmas gifts for his family, Al works as a mall Santa Claus; he is teased by Marcy and Jefferson.

13. Jan. 10, 1993. "Wedding Show"
A cousin of Al's is about to get married. Peg cannot decide what to wear. She dresses and re-dresses while Al stresses. Worse, Bud gets much too close to his cousin's fiancée!

14. Jan. 24, 1993. "It Doesn't Get Any Better Than This"
Peg and Marcy join Al on a fishing trip. Kelly, Bud, and Seven get together with Jefferson to splurge with Marcy's money.

15. Feb. 7, 1993. "Heels on Wheels"
Kelly feels depressed at being a diner server and decides to assert herself by getting a motorcycle. Her mom and dad also enjoy the bike.

16. Feb. 14, 1993. "Mr. Empty Pants"
Peg draws a caricature of Al that brings him fame as "Mr. Empty Pants."

17. Feb. 21, 1993. "You Can't Miss"
Desperate for a date, Bud is accepted on a TV dating game program entitled "You Can't Miss."

18. Feb. 28, 1993. "Peggy and the Pirates"
Peg tells Seven a bedtime story that is shown as her fantasy about pirates. Each character in the fantasy is modeled on a major *MWC* character and played by that character's actor.

19. Mar. 14, 1993. "Go for the Old"
Al is happy to get into a film theater as a senior citizen, but it later makes him worry about aging.

20. Mar. 28, 1993. "Un-Alful Entry"
A burglar breaks into the Bundy residence. Al socks the man and kicks him out of the house. Then the burglar sues Al!

21. Apr. 11, 1993. "Movie Show"
Kelly is depressed after a break-up with a boyfriend, so the other members of the family try to cheer her up by treating her to a movie.

22. **Apr. 25, 1993. "'Til Death Do Us Part"**
Upset that the neighborhood laughs about his lackluster sexual skills, Al tries to get in shape.

23. **May 2, 1993. "'Tis Time to Smell the Roses"**
Al takes $12,000 to retire but Peg splurges with the money. Al goes back to the shoe store and is excited by the presentation of an opportunity for him to buy his own shoe store.

24. **May 9, 1993. "Old Insurance Dodge"**
The Bundy Dodge is stolen and Al tries to cheat the insurance company.

25. **May 16, 1993. "The Wedding Repercussions"**
Bud's cousin just learned that his new wife cheated on him. Bud is terrified that the large, strong man will find out Bud is the man who bedded the bride.

26. **May 23, 1993. "The Proposition"**
A wealthy woman has the hots for Al and offers the family half a million dollars for him.

SEASON 8

1. **Sept. 5, 1993. "A Tisket, a Tasket, Can Peg Make a Basket?"**
Peg insists on accompanying Al when he gets tickets to a basketball game. She is chosen for a $10,000 free throw contest!

2. **Sept. 12, 1993. "Hood in the Boyz"**
A childhood friend asks for Al's help in dealing with a young punk who is harassing her at her convenience store job.

3. **Sept. 19, 1993. "Proud to be Your Bud?"**
The other Bundys fear Bud has gone insane when they hear him talking in the basement with an alter ego.

4. **Sept. 26, 1993. "Luck of the Bundys"**
Kelly is again The Verminator. The Bundys appear to be enjoying good luck which concerns Al because it is so un-Bundy-like.

5. **Oct. 3, 1993. "Banking on Marcy"**
   Marcy is afraid to speak in public. Talking to a meeting of bankers, she super-embarrasses Peg and Jefferson with a public orgasm.

6. **Oct. 10, 1993. "No Chicken, No Check"**
   Kelly and Bud together buy a car but each wants time alone with a date and wants the other plus the other's date out.

7. **Oct. 24, 1993. "Take My Wife, Please"**
   It is Halloween and Al meets the Grim Reaper—in the form of a black-haired Peg.

8. **Nov. 7, 1993. "Scared Single"**
   Aaron comes to work in the shoe store. Al is afraid for Aaron, who is engaged, so Al counsels him that marriage leads to suffering.

9. **Nov. 14, 1993. "NO MA'AM"**
   Al and his male friends get upset at what they see as female encroachment into male areas and form an organization called NO MA'AM.

10. **Nov. 21, 1993. "Dances with Weezie"**
    Al and Jefferson plot to avoid accompanying Peg and Marcy to a reunion event for *The Jeffersons*. The two men want to attend the opening of a sports bar.

11. **Nov. 28, 1993. "Change for a Buck"**
    Buck runs away from home because he feels neglected by the Bundys. He finds himself in a shelter in which he will be killed if someone does not take him home within seven days.

12. **Dec. 12, 1993. "A Little Off the Top"**
    Al is injured and in the hospital given the wrong treatment: a circumcision.

13. **Dec. 19, 1993. "The Worst Noel"**
    Bud and Kelly attempt to sneak a Christmas present for Al and Peg, a jukebox, into the house without Al and Peg knowing about it.

14. **Jan. 16, 1994. "Sofa So Good"**
    While Al and Peg are away, Kelly's date destroys the Bundy sofa. Kelly finds the maker of the couch, now a crazed hermit, and tries to wheedle a duplicate from him.

15. **Jan. 23, 1994. "Honey, I Blew Myself Up"**
    A photographer hangs a sensuous photograph of Peg on the wall outside the shoe store. Al wants to get it down without telling Peg that having other men look at it makes him jealous.

16. **Feb. 6, 1994. "How Green Was My Apple"**
    The Bundys and D'Arcys battle over possession of an apple tree and other items on disputed property around their houses.

17. **Feb. 13, 1994. "Valentine's Day Massacre"**
    Al does last minute shopping for a Valentine's gift for Peg, frantically battling other similarly situated men. Bud seeks a girl who sent him a Valentine's Day card years ago that Kelly forgot to show him until recently.

18. **Feb. 20, 1994. "Get Outta Dodge"**
    Because there is almost one million miles on the odometer of Al's Dodge, he gets an offer for a brand-new Viper from Dodge, providing they film his Dodge actually crossing the million mark.

19. **Feb. 27, 1994. "Field of Screams"**
    Al protests the destruction of his old high school football field to build an auto plant by chaining himself to a goalpost.

20. **Mar. 20, 1994. "The D'Arcy Files"**
    A man offers Al a reward for the capture of Jefferson, said to be a spy against America. Is this an April Fool's joke?

21. **Apr. 10, 1994. "Nooner or Nothing"**
    Peg tries to get Al to meet the requirements of a radio game show without telling him that he is in a contest.

22. **Apr. 24, 1994. "Ride Scare"**
    Al ends up carpooling with three plus-sized lingerie models

23. May 1, 1994. "The Legend of Ironhead Haynes"
Al leads the NO MA'AM crew to search for a legendary macho man, nicknamed Ironhead Haynes, said to now be living in the mountains.

24. May 8, 1994. "Assault and Batteries"
Al hopes to fix a cellar step before his beloved *Hondo* comes on TV. When he tries to buy batteries for his flashlight, he finds himself locked inside the store.

25. May 15, 1994. "Al Goes Deep"
Al bets on a football game. One of the most important players gets a crush on Kelly; Al is dismayed because he wants the footballer to focus on football.

26. May 22, 1994. "Kelly Knows Something"
Al tries out for a TV show sports trivia game show. He is not accepted but Kelly is. Can Al fill her with enough sports trivia to make a winner of her?

SEASON 9

1. Sept. 4, 1994. "Shoeway to Heaven"
Al and Jefferson hold a special shoe sale with a 1970s-nostalgia theme.

2. Sept. 11, 1994. "Driving Mr. Boondy"
Bud gets a job as a driving examiner. Al is stunned to find out his son will be Al's driving examiner.

3. Sept. 18, 1994. "Kelly Breaks Out"
Desperate to rid herself of a pimple, Kelly uses a zit removal cream that leaves her bald-headed and bearded!

4. Sept. 25, 1994. "Naughty but Niece"
Marcy's sweet and sexy niece Amber visits. Horny Bud is unsure whether their encounters are real or dreamed.

4. **Oct. 2, 1994. "Business Sucks, Pt. 1"**
   Al insists a breastfeeding mother leave the shoe store. Marcy and her group protest.

5. **Oct. 9, 1994. "Business Still Sucks, Pt. 2"**
   Al and NO MA'AM stage a counter protest in which they whip off their shirts to expose their beer bellies.

6. **Oct. 16, 1994. "Dial B for Virgin"**
   Bud is mortified to find that his college community service assignment is to volunteer for a phone line that encourages virgins to remain sexually inexperienced.

7. **Oct. 23, 1994. "Sleepless in Chicago"**
   Jefferson is shocked to find that he bought a Barbie doll for Marcy that is worth a small fortune. He asks Al to sleep next to Marcy while Jefferson goes somewhere to exchange dolls.

8. **Nov. 6, 1994. "No Pot to Pease In"**
   TV producers take stories Kelly has told about her family and write a sitcom script around those stories.

9. **Nov. 13, 1994. "Dud Bowl"**
   A man who went to a school that was a rival to Polk High challenges Al and other alumni to see who could win a football game. Middle-aged men, including some ex-pros snuck into the team that is the Polk rival, face off in a football match.

10. **Nov. 27, 1994. "A Man for No Seasons"**
    Pro baseball players go on strike and the NO MA'AM bunch form their own league.

11. **Dec. 11, 1994. "I Want My Psycho Dad, Pt. 1"**
    Marcy's group gets *Psycho Dad* taken off TV. Al leads a NO MA'AM protest to bring it back.

12. **Dec. 18, 1994. "I Want My Psycho Dad: Second Blood, Pt. 2"**
    NO MA'AM goes to Washington D.C. to testify before Congress in hopes of bringing *Psycho Dad* back.

13. Jan. 8, 1995. "The Naked and the Dead, But Mostly the Naked"
Peg and other neighborhood wives accompany Al and other neighborhood husbands to The Jiggly Room.

14. Jan. 15, 1995. "Kelly Takes a Shot"
Kelly tries to learn archery for an audition.

15. Feb. 5, 1995. "Best of Bundy"
Title self-explanatory: A roundup of the show's best moments.

16. Feb. 5, 1995. "Get the Dodge Outta Hell"
Al is upset to find that his Dodge has mysteriously disappeared when taken to the local carwash.

17. Feb. 12, 1995. "25 Years and What Do You Get?"
Getting old and addled, Buck buried in the backyard the necklace that Al had bought for Peg and intended to give her for their 25th anniversary.

18. Feb. 19, 1995. "Ship Happens, Pt. 1"
Peg wins a cruise. She takes along not only Al but the D'Arcys.

19. Feb. 26, 1995. "Ship Happens, Pt. 2"
The ship sinks. Al, Peg, Marcy, and Jefferson find themselves on the little life raft with comedian Gilbert Gottfried and a fat lady.

20. Mar. 12, 1995. "Something Larry This Way Comes"
Kelly attends the Larry Storch School of Acting and is chosen to appear in a Phantom of the Opera production opposite Storch. Shoe storeowner Gary knocks Storch out. Can the show go on?

21. Mar. 26, 1995. "And Bingo Was Her Game-O"
Peg is invited to the Bingo Invitational Final.

22. Apr. 9, 1995. "User Friendly"
Bud becomes obsessed with a virtual reality experiment he hopes will rejuvenate his sex life.

23. Apr. 30, 1995. "Pump Fiction"
Kelly and Al together make a documentary film about shoes for an assignment in Kelly's class in the Larry Storch School of Acting. This was followed by a special, "My Favorite Married," in which the main cast members talked about their favorite moments from the series.

24. May 7, 1995. "Radio Free Trumaine"
A spin-off pilot in which Steve Rhoades, now a college official, expels two flamboyant college radio disc jockeys.

25. May 14, 1995. "Shoeless Al"
The shoe store is robbed and Al is tied up. He sues the mall, claiming the trauma left him unable to even be around shoes.

26. May 21, 1995. "The Undergraduate"
Kelly's secret admirer turns out to be 12 years old! He is the son of the man who owns the company at which Kelly is employed, so she allows the child to take her to the Junior Prom despite knowing they make a ludicrous "couple."

SEASON 10

1. Sept. 17, 1995. "Guess Who's Coming to Breakfast, Lunch and Dinner"
Peg's grotesquely obese mother—who is never seen by the audience—moves into the Bundy house.

2. Sept. 24, 1995. "A Shoe Room with a View"
At the suggestion of Al and Griff, Gary has a room adjacent to the shoe store turned into an aerobics studio. Al and friends eagerly peep into holes to watch the action but, instead of the young *Playboy*-centerfold types they anticipated, they see fat women!

3. Oct. 1, 1995 . "Requiem for a Dead Briard"
Buck dies. He is reincarnated as Lucky and finds himself once again the dog of the Bundys.

4. Oct. 8, 1995 . "Reverend Al"
To enjoy tax benefits, NO MA'AM becomes a religion.

5. Oct. 15, 1995. "How Bleen Was My Kelly"
Kelly inadvertently creates "Bleen," a formula causing extreme hair growth.

6. Oct. 22, 1995. "The Weaker Sex"
Peg does so well in her self-defense class that Al feels threatened.

7. Oct. 29, 1995. "Flight of the Bumblebee"
Bud must get a photograph taken of him with professional wrestler King Kong Bundy to gain admittance to NO MA'AM.

8. Nov. 5, 1995. "Blonde and Blonder"
Marcy organizes a "Toys for Guns" campaign against toy guns. Kelly learns a nerd she once viewed contemptuously has grown up to become not only handsome, but wealthy.

9. Nov. 19, 1995. "The Two That Got Away"
Al and Jefferson arrive at a fishing lodge to be told to leave because blonde beauty and former *Playboy* model Shannon Tweed has taken their reservation.

10. Nov. 26, 1995. "Dud Bowl II"
Al hopes a new Polk High scoreboard will be named after him but discovers plans are underway to name it after NFL pro Terry Bradshaw. This episode was followed by "Al Bundy Sports Spectacular."

11. Dec. 3, 1995. "Bearly Men"
To prove their manliness, Al and Bud bring back a dead bear from the woods. Then the bear, which was just hibernating, wakes up!

12. Dec. 10, 1995. "Love Conquers All"
Kelly suffers bitter disappointment when she dates handsome Carlos and finds he treats her with respect rather than lust.

13. Dec. 17, 1995. "I Can't Believe It's Butter"
Griff becomes enamored of telephone sex worker "Butter." Al is horrified when he discovers that Butter is Peg's mother.

14. Jan. 7, 1996. "The Hood, The Bud & The Kelly, Pt. 1"
After purchasing a satellite dish, Al and Jefferson endure multiple perils as they try to install it. Bud borrows money from a gangster to bankroll an exercise video starring Kelly and a handsome man.

15. Jan. 14, 1996. "The Hood, The Bud & The Kelly, Pt. 2"
The gangster's crony warns Bud that he better get the video done soon or he will face horrible consequences. However, Kelly and the man with whom she is working quarrel incessantly because each wants to be the video's star.

16. Feb. 4, 1996. "Calendar Girl"
Bud wants to make a *Girls of Trumaine* calendar.

17. Feb. 11, 1996. "The Agony and the Extra C"
On the D'Arcys' wedding anniversary, Jefferson is laid up in the hospital. Talking with Bud and Kelly, Jefferson describes a trauma that began when he and the rest of NO MA'AM were at The Nudie Bar.

18. Feb. 18, 1996. "Spring Break, Pt. 1"
Bud and the three other guys in his group have their tickets to the Spring Break in Fort Lauderdale hornswoggled from them by Kelly and three of her gal-pals.

19. Feb. 25, 1996. "Spring Break, Pt. 2"
Marcy leads Bud and the nerds on a trek to Fort Lauderdale for revenge.

20. Mar. 17, 1996. "Turning Japanese"
Marcy needs to impress her Japanese boss to get a promotion. She knows having the Bundys as her next-door neighbors is not good for a positive impression and wants them to decamp as long as the boss is around.

21. Mar. 24, 1996. "Al Goes to the Dogs"
Al makes a lot of noise as he builds a doghouse for Lucky. Marcy gets a building inspector to cause Al trouble.

22. Apr. 14, 1996. "Enemies"
Pilot for a proposed series, it concerns a conflicted group of sometime friends (and enemies).

23. Apr. 28, 1996. "Bud Hits the Books"
Horny and frustrated, Bud needs to study and attempts to avoid anything that could possibly remind him of sex. Needless to say, this is a daunting task.

24. May 5, 1996. "Kiss of the Coffee Woman"
Marcy tells Jefferson he must find a job before she will let him in the house. He gets a job playing in a commercial opposite Kelly. A script says they must kiss.

25. May 19, 1996. "Torch Song Duet"
Griff wins a radio contest so he can carry the Olympic torch.

26. May 19, 1996. "The Joke's on Al"
NO MA'AM members play practical jokes on each other. The worst prank is played on Griff, who is arrested as a murderer and cannibal.

SEASON 11

1. Sept. 28, 1996. "Twisted"
Bud is attracted to a girl who is sexually excited by danger.

2. Oct. 5, 1996. "Children of the Corns"
Al learns that Gary is running an illegal sweatshop.

3. Oct. 12, 1996. "Kelly's Gotta Habit"
To be the TV commercial spokesperson for an olive oil made by nuns, Kelly must abstain from sex.

4. Nov. 10, 1996. "Requiem for a Chevyweight, Pt. 1"
Al has great difficulty getting the Dodge to work. However, he does not want to part with it because so many memories are attached to the vehicle.

5. Nov. 17, 1996. "Requiem for a Chevyweight, Pt. 2"
Al orchestrates a "funeral" for the "dead" Dodge and buries it in the backyard. Peg wants to sell its spare parts.

6. Nov. 24, 1996. "A Bundy Thanksgiving"
Al wants the family to enjoy his Aunt Maddie's potato pie for Thanksgiving, but finds she has just died. Jefferson seeks a turkey for Marcy and wants the stray turkey that followed Kelly home.

7. Dec. 1, 1996. "The Juggs Have Left the Building"
The Bundys vacation in Branson, Missouri where Peg and Kelly appear onstage in a country music contest. They also meet Tammy Wynette. Marcy and Jefferson do sexual role-playing as Peg and Al.

8. Dec. 22, 1996. "God Help Ye Merry Bundymen"
Gary fires Al and Griff at Christmastime and they take bizarre and embarrassing jobs in the mall. However, Gary eventually re-hires them.

9. Dec. 29, 1996. "Crimes Against Obesity"
A group of fat ladies whom Al has insulted gather together to put him on trial for repeatedly offending the heavyset.

10. Jan. 6, 1997. "The Stepford Peg"
Peg hits her head and gets amnesia. Al "brainwashes" her into becoming a super-domestic, super-industrious type of housewife.

11. Jan. 13, 1997. "Bud on the Side"
Shoestore owner Gary and Bud start dating.

12. Jan. 20, 1997. "Grime and Punishment"
Al begins charging Bud rent. A health inspector declares the basement condemned and gives Al a month to make appropriate repairs.

13. Jan. 27, 1997. "T*R*A*S*H*"
Jefferson joins the National Guard and regales Al and Griff with perks for being in the National Guard, such as getting paid to party! Al and Griff want to join just to get in on the fun Jefferson describes.

14. Feb. 24, 1997. "Breaking Up Is Easy to Do, Pt. 1"
In a party game, couples test their knowledge of their partners. Peg is outraged that Al has apparently forgotten their most romantic evening.

15. Feb 24, 1997. "Breaking Up Is Easy to Do, Pt. 2"
Al moves out. Peg sinks into depression as the kids look for a stepdad, and Al attempts to become a swinging bachelor.

16. Mar. 3, 1997. "Breaking Up Is Easy to Do, Pt. 3"
Peg and Al reconcile, realizing they are meant for each other.

17. Mar. 10, 1997. "Live Nude Peg"
Peg tries out at The Jiggly Room, dressed as a "harem girl," complete with veil over her face. Al does not realize it is Peg and finds the "harem girl" entrancing.

18. Mar. 17, 1997. "A Babe in Toyland"
Kelly tastes success in a children's show and it goes to her head so Bud resolves to teach her a lesson.

19. Mar. 31, 1997. "Birthday Boy Toy"
Jefferson turns 40 and Marcy demands he get a job. He is hired as an aerobics teacher.

20. Apr. 28, 1997. "Damn Bundys"
Al sells his soul to Lucifer so he can play pro football for the Bears.

21. Apr. 10, 1997. "Lez Be Friends"
Marcy's cousin Mandy visits. Peg and Marcy are jealous of the attention Al and Jefferson pay to Mandy, until they learn she is a lesbian.

22. May 5, 1997. "The Desperate Half-Hour"
The Bundys are taken hostage by a pen pal of Bud's who has escaped from prison

23. May 5, 1997. "How to Marry a Moron"
Kelly is about to marry when she discovers her fiancé has been cheating.

24. Jun. 9, 1997. "Chicago Shoe Exchange"
Al and Griff barter shoes for wanted items. Kelly wants to become a massage therapist and disables Bud when she practices her newfound "skills" on him.

www.ingramcontent.com/pod-product-compliance
Lightning Source LLC
Chambersburg PA
CBHW072158160426
43197CB00012B/2439